MW00527072

See Me Grieve

A Widow's Journey

E. A. TOBOLSKI

Ten|16
PRESS
www.ten16press.com - Waukesha, WI

Half of the royalties for this book will be donated to the Restoring Hope & Peace grant through the Hope for Widows Foundation. The Hope for Widows Foundation is a philanthropic not-for-profit organization, developed by widowed women, that strives to build community among widowed women. For more information about them and their programs, visit www.hopeforwidows.org.

See Me Grieve
Copyrighted © 2021 E. A. Tobolski
ISBN 9781645382478
First Edition

See Me Grieve
by E. A. Tobolski

All Rights Reserved. Written permission must be secured from the publisher to use or reproduce any part of this book, except for brief quotations in critical reviews or articles.

For information, please contact:

www.ten16press.com
Waukesha, WI

Edited by Jenna Zerbel
Cover design by Kaeley Dunteman

Page 45: Painting © Rachel Parker, https://www.rachelsstudio.com/
Page 249: Photo © Lisa Howard

The author has made every effort to ensure that the information within this book was accurate at the time of publication. The author does not assume and hereby disclaims any liability to any party for any loss, damage, or disruption caused by errors or omissions, whether such errors or omissions result from accident, negligence, or any other cause.

To Beth, Maryann, Rose, and Terri, my best friends and gentlest pillars. Thank you for picking up me off the ground and helping me stand again.

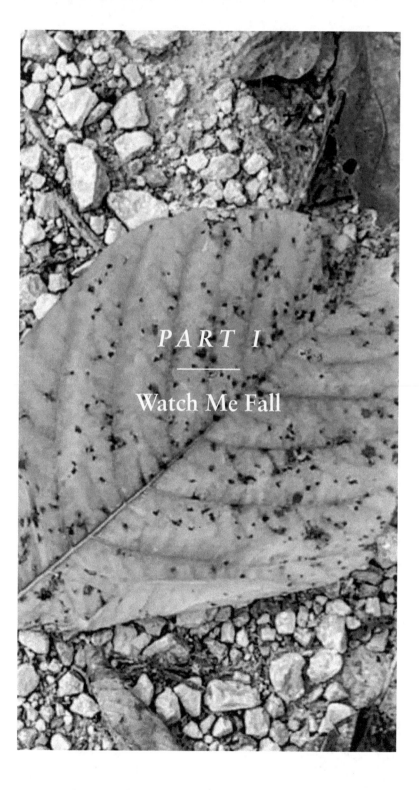

PART I

Watch Me Fall

And So It Begins

Not everyone will understand documenting in words what life is like without my husband of twenty-eight years, my friend for thirty-two. Some may even judge me for it, thinking it inappropriate to write about my life after my husband's sudden death in a motorcycle accident ten days ago. But I am a writer, so I write. If I were a runner, I'd run, or a swimmer, I'd swim. In my mind right now, I picture my husband chuckling at these two analogies, as he would know I am neither of those things. I am a writer, a writer with a heart exposed on my sleeve for all to see. I struggle to hide any of my emotions. I can see Peter nod in agreement to this admission.

The details of my husband's death aren't necessary. The specifics are too muddled and painful to think about anyway. The initial report seems to point the blame at the other driver. Not sure yet what the official report will conclude—that's going to take some time. And I suppose it doesn't matter where the fault lies right now; maybe it will in a month when I can direct my anger somewhere, to someone. For now, all I know, all I feel, is my husband is dead, and I must start the last part of my life without him. We were supposed to travel on that path together. Supposed-to's aren't what actually happens.

And now, in the past few days, I've been living in a fog. Sometimes it lifts, sometimes it stays, too dense to see right in front of me, and most times it's clear enough to navigate with fear and caution. I got the mundane things out of the way—planning the memorial service, breaking the news to family and friends, letting his workplace know, taking care of necessary paperwork, talking to insurance companies, and going through some of his things. Peter kept a lot of things. As much as he was the organizer in our relationship, he was also the keeper of crap, always explaining, "One day I may use it." In his defense, he used some, but not all. In his defense, I am now scrambling to find the warranties, the sale receipts I didn't keep, the ones I need this morning.

After days of taking care of the banal and the necessary, with poor sleep interrupted by ruminations in constant motion, yesterday was a day to sleep. I finally slept, really slept. I slept one night going into the next day and napped most of the next day. My adrenaline sprung a leak, and I collapsed. I wish I could say it felt good. Maybe it would have if I didn't wake up to the same nightmare, the reality of Peter's death. Sleep didn't take away the emptiness or the dread inside of me. All it did was push it back.

Every day, there is some anthill or mountain to conquer. The anthills are easy. The mountains make it hard to catch my breath. It was so much easier to climb both with my husband at my side. Easier is not in the game plan now. I have to write a new one. It'll be okay. I am a writer, you know.

Mowing and Hemsworth Didn't Do It For Me

Yesterday had its moments. I grew impatient with the people from Peter's motorcycle insurance company. They bounced me around and around, each time saying, "I'm sorry for your loss." Why do people say, "Sorry for your loss"? It's not like I'll ever find him again. He's gone. I know they mean well, but I think a better wording would be, "Sorry for your pain," or, "Sorry he's gone." But I digress. Afterwards, the fourth person I spoke with assured me I would be getting a phone call. That never happened. I may expose this insurance company soon if they don't get their act together. I received terrible customer service, especially as a person who recently had half of herself cut out.

After the motorcycle debacle, I called to cancel our subscription to a newspaper. *Our* subscription. Who am I kidding? It was Peter's subscription. My husband was old school and loved to read the paper every day, cover to cover. I get my information from internet newsfeeds or articles online. But Peter? He read it all. I explained to the representative that I wanted to end our subscription and choked up about how the newspaper was my husband's love, not mine. She asked if I wished to subscribe to just the weekend edition. I mean, I get it. She was doing her job. But I just told her, with tears, it was my husband's love.

I kind of snapped at her and asked if she needed me to repeat myself. She said no, apologized for "my loss," and I hung up after telling her, "I shouldn't have snapped."

Next, I cut the back lawn. I mowed for years and loved it until Peter took the chore over. His engineering mind didn't always like the unpredictable "patterns" I made in the grass. As I mowed, I walked past the lilac bushes he planted for me because he knew it was my favorite scent. I saw the overgrown pumpkin vines he sowed in the spring because he knew I wanted them for decorations in the fall. And I smiled at the lilies he planted this year for me because they were our wedding flowers. Peter wasn't much in words of affection, but boy, that man could show his love. All of this and more made me miss him, love him, and cry for him. The serenity I enjoyed with mowing took a more reflective path on Peter, his absence in my life, and the finality of his death. I felt empty.

Finally, my two adult children and I went to see *Men in Black*. I wanted to go as a way to numb my mind. I thought a semi-comedy with the beautiful Chris Hemsworth in it would certainly be a distraction. Only it wasn't. I cried through a movie intended to make me laugh. I didn't ugly-cry or sob. The tears I shed came down silently in a slow, steady leak of a stream. In the darkness of the theater, I felt the never-again's. Never again will I hold his hand while watching a movie. Never again will I make snide comments to him during an awful scene. Never again will he laugh at me because I laughed so hard, too hard, at a stupid pun in the movie. Never again will we be at the theater together. Never-again's are replacing our always-did's. And that wasn't fair. That wasn't right. That was too much.

When we got home, my daughter and son went off to do their siblings-things. My brother once told me the closest person we are to anyone by blood is a sibling, and my daughter and son needed to share their unique closeness. I sat down and had a good, proper cry before I exploded in multiple texts to my people, the women who have held me up and let me fall into crumbles. The women who I needed, still need, will always need. In a flurry of texts to them, I described my awful day of mowing and Hemsworth.

Today is Not a Day for Fighting

Today, I am exhausted—mind, body, and soul. I am exhausted because I just can't deal with all the fighting I have to do with insurance companies, with social security, with . . . well, it's a long list. Part of it is on me. Some things can wait, but waiting is not me. I lost a lot of me when Peter died, but some things remained, and impatience is one of them. And today, from all the fights, I've been knocked down.

I'll admit, I'm lying on the mat, and I could stay down. I could lie in my bed all day, and no one would blame me. Yet, for me, the only thing that accomplishes is a sore hip and back. I could let the house and finances go, not make phone calls, walk around with a stench from lack of showering and hair washings, and eat ice cream bars all day as I stare into space. I could. I really could. My stubborn fight in me, the one encouraging me not to give up, pushes me to move, act, and not surrender to a knockout.

My husband's memory, and all I know he would have wanted from me, keeps me from that eight count. Peter's tenacious nature showed me I could do anything. It's his energetic spirit that never slowed down, and it encourages me to keep moving. And it's my determined spirit of strength, if not for me, then for my kids and my incredible

group of terrific women that keep me from defeat, from
whiffing the smelling salt.

But today, I am exhausted. The spirits inside me need to
rest, which means I cannot see my beloved mother today.
I wanted to see her. I haven't seen her since Peter died. My
family members tell me she understands Peter died, or at
least she did yesterday. My mom also thinks she attended
the memorial services. She did not because my mother is
not physically capable of attending anything. It doesn't
stop her from retelling stories as if she were there. I know
she loved Peter very much. I know, in her own way, in
her own mind, she misses him. A hug from her would
be welcomed today or at any point. Yet I know seeing
her would also mean feeling disappointed because she
isn't able to be the mother I need her to be for me. I also
know I would battle with my impatience as she tells her
stories that are real to only her. And the guilt with both is
something I cannot bear today, a day where I know, I need
rest, a day which means avoiding any battles and giving in
to my exhaustion.

The Be-Bitching Hour

Last night, I became a bitch. It's not something most people plan to do; it happens. It happens to me, and most likely others, for various reasons—lack of sleep, too much sleep, stress, illness, not enough caffeine, too much caffeine, the list can go on and on. Last night, I morphed into one because of jealousy and uncertainty.

The day was going fine as I slept through most of it. It's been my routine. One day I'm okay; the next day, all I want to do is sleep. And it's not even good sleep. It's enough to make time go by faster, in hopes for this nightmare to end. Even though I know trying to time travel through sleep won't accomplish anything, I still try to jump to the ending chapters.

Last night, my son, my daughter, and I had dinner out before my daughter headed back to her home and career five hours away. She needs to go back. I want her to go back. My husband would have wanted her to go back. Her life has to continue, not stand still. She's too young and talented for her to remain sedentary.

We walked to a local brewery. Because of its proximity to my home, it's a place I could escape if I felt the need to leave. As we headed toward a table all the way in the back of the restaurant, one I chose for privacy in case any tears came, I stopped to say hello to friends celebrating birthdays. One of the friends has been so kind to me, and the others are plain kind. As we continued our walk to our table, we walked past a group of men howling in laughter about something. We sat down near a table of a mother and father correcting their children's manners. Not far from us was a table of girlfriends sharing stories. A few tables away sat a pregnant woman finishing off the leftovers on her husband's and daughter's plates. It made me smile, remembering my own pregnancies.

Our dinner was fine. The fried cheese curds were amazing. I'm not much into beer, but it was refreshing on a ninety-one-degree day. My daughter entertained us with her always engaging and humorous stories. My son threw in an anecdote here and there, but like his father, he is a man of few words, especially surrounded by my daughter and me. The two of us tend to talk a lot.

Usually, I would have quips, stories of my own, and talk with the server. (It's a tough job, one I did for a while in my college years. Servers don't always get seen, and I try my best to see them.) "Usually" is a thing of the past now. Instead, I sat stoic, knowing what was about to come. See, when the day strikes five o'clock in the evening, dread, depression, anxiety, and all of the above rob me of speech and enjoyment and replace those things with the ugly parts of myself.

Before we left, I went to the restroom. As I washed my hands, I fell forward and gripped the lip of the sink. I saw my wedding ring on my finger, and Peter's next to it, the one I placed there in the hospital sitting next to his dead body. I gulped down deep breaths of air, trying to hold off my rising panic.

I let the panic and its tears come once we left the restaurant and walked home. Tears came from the fear of permanently taking off the wedding rings one day. They came from hating that my days were no longer regular days of celebrating birthdays, laughing with girlfriends, and being part of the conversation. They came from loneliness already felt from my daughter heading back to her life and leaving me, alone, in mine. And they came from the hour, the be-bitching hour that has struck every night since Peter died.

When I got home, I texted friends about how down I was and about the question of my wedding ring. I included rants on how unfair it was that the celebrations, the laughing it up, the families together, and the chatter of a Saturday evening were still happening while I was in deep despair. In the light of today, I know, of course, life goes on, and it should. After five o'clock, I will block out any reasoning because my life goes on more sadly.

After texting my friends, I flipped through social media and saw a beautiful picture of a lake a person posted. The caption read something like, *"God is always good."* Like a full moon changing a person into a werewolf, the snapshot officially turned me into a bitch. I commented, *"I don't see it that way,"* as if I needed to ruin her moment. I even texted a *"Could you believe so and so wrote this on Facebook while my life is crap?"* to two of my friends. They didn't have my back on this one, just an understanding, *"Things are tough right now,"* response.

The other night, as I lay in bed, I thought about my be-bitching hours. Five o'clock was the hour my routine with Peter would begin. The hour when he came home from work, and I had dinner ready so we could sit to talk about our days. Afterward, I washed the dinner dishes, and he put away the food. The hours continued with Peter sitting down to read his newspaper or play his ukulele as I would flip through the television. The day would end with us giving the other a kiss goodnight and knowing another day would begin tomorrow. Now, this routine is gone, and all our tomorrows no longer exist. So, the be-bitching hour strikes, and the bitch in me comes out, angry as hell because I no longer have any of it, and I miss all of it.

Never a Good Cry

Yesterday was not a good day. I went through the motions of waking up, making phone calls, doing some paperwork, staring at laundry baskets full of clean clothes waiting to be folded for days, even getting out to run errands—small, close-to-the-house errands. My son came over in the afternoon for about three hours. We talked and shared a dinner of blueberry pancakes and bacon, neither foods I particularly like much but craved yesterday for some unknown reason. And even though I kept busy— well, my version of busy lately—I fought with the bad day.

I pushed myself through the conversation, dinner with my son, and a phone call with my daughter. I held back most of my tears, not wanting to let them go until I was alone. I have the most compassionate kids—great huggers, too—but I wanted to mourn privately yesterday, which is odd since death is never between just two people. It has a ripple effect that never quite ends with only two people, yet the pull to be alone to release my tears was greater yesterday than any other day in recent days. When my son left, I finally broke into hard, deep, gut-wrenching sobs, and I didn't stop for over an hour. When it slowed, I hiccupped with more. I had what they call a *"good cry."*

Good cries are oxymorons. It's like saying I had a *"bad laugh."* There's nothing good about a cry. Oh, some people think a long, steely cry can make you feel better with the release. And yes, there have been times I have felt better. Though, during it, there's nothing good going on. Eventually—and in my case, there will be many more eventually's—I'll cry again and for new and old reasons. Yesterday, when day turned to night, at the time of day that always brings me to my knees, I wept because I knew Peter wasn't on vacation or a business trip or late getting home. Yesterday, like the fright you feel when a rollercoaster dips, I knew Peter was gone forever. He was dead.

In these past weeks, I experienced great sadness. When it was too much, I sprinkled my thoughts with an unhealthy but reassuring dose of *Peter will be home soon*. I pulled these thoughts out of reserve when I felt most depleted. But yesterday, the last hope of Peter coming home soon left me forever. I had nothing to believe in anymore.

As I cried, my shouts of *it's not fair* echoed in my empty living room, one I no longer shared with Peter. I clutched my belly in pain, trying to keep down the blueberry pancakes. I cried and screamed, and then did both some more.

A friend messaged me offering to go for a walk together. I refused, knowing a mess of a person walking down the street would not do any good. Two neighbors let me know they were thinking of me, and another friend, one I don't see often, sent an, *"I'm thinking of you tonight,"* text. And I talked, for over an hour, with one of my besties who eventually got me to laugh. When I went to bed, I was exhausted from the *"good cry,"* and my sleep was fitful.

There was nothing *"good"* about my cry last night. Mine were sobs of releasing any hope of his return or a life resuming together. They were tears of *why me?*, of *I'm scared*, of *how can I keep on keeping on without him?*, of *I miss him*, and, of course, of *he's never coming back*. Last night, I cried because I finally faced the harshest reality and the saddest truth. Peter is never coming back, and there was nothing good in any of those tears.

Oh, God!

I've always believed in God. From an early age, I spoke to God, prayed to God, worshiped, and thanked God. I grew up a staunch Catholic. I attended Catholic schools for fourteen years until I transferred to a state university to finish my college degree. My father was one of the first deacons with the Catholic church. I attended Mass, received the sacraments, and made sure my children did the same. I said the rosary, read books or articles on saints, and I kept my faith front and center in my life.

Of course, as I grew older, my perception of God and religion changed and then changed again, but I always remained a believer. I am not, nor have I ever been, pious. I would instead use the word spiritual to describe me. I did go through a phase in my early twenties, where I thought of becoming a nun. I think many Catholics think about going into a vocation for a minute or two.

About ten years ago, I converted to another religion. I still held tight to my belief in God and my faith in Her/His/Their teachings. Heck, I even wrote thankful letters to God every Sunday on Facebook. Spirituality, belief, and religion remained a huge part of who I was, even if I stopped going into a building every Sunday. God was a part of my definition of myself. The night Peter died, everything changed.

My perception of God was formulated by perhaps well-meaning nuns. Early on, I learned anything I did or said God recorded and would go over with me after I died. If I put extra money into those Lenten donation cans for a missionary, God would be pleased. If I took money out of those cans to buy candy, God would be displeased. If I liked a boy and remained coy, God smiled down on me. If I French-kissed a boy, I sinned and would have to atone in the afterlife. Everything I did affected God's perception of me.

I also learned everything happening in life was God's will. It was God's will if a hamster, a classmate, or a parent died. Natural disasters were God's will. If some people were more impoverished than others, God preordained it. If I didn't win a speech contest, a softball game, a boy's attention, God predetermined it. God had Her/His/Their hand in every outcome of my life. To learn all this as an already-anxious child not only placed guilt in me, but it also formed my fearful image of God. I perceived God as always tallying, always judging, and always controlling.

These perceptions stayed with me as the years went on. I continued to look toward God as the ultimate controller and the zenith in tally-taking events in my life, in anyone's life. Oh, sure, I knew it was ridiculous, especially reading and listening to others' views on God as I grew older. Still, it's what I kept coming back to, and when Peter died so suddenly, I was, I am, not only pissed off at God, but I also mourn the loss of two important parts of me—the one Peter held and my faith.

The biggest question I keep asking is why God took Peter. Why did God take him from my life, from my children's lives, especially when my ninety-one-year-old mother pleads to leave this world? If God needed to take a life, why not my mother's well-lived one, the one ready to spend eternity with Her/Him/Them and all the people who died before her, including my father? Why take the life of a man who still wanted to do so much more? What was God's purpose in all of this?

Don't get me wrong. I love my mother with my entire heart. I love her so much that I want her to be happy, and for my mother, a godly woman who taught me spirituality through her unselfishness and commitment, saying goodbye to this world to join God is what will make her happy. She has told me this many of times in the past few years. Peter and I discussed our future, our empty-nest-ready-for-retirement future. It makes no sense. It wipes away any view I held of God's love for me, my kids, and my mother. Peter's death goes against my formative lessons of God that still linger in me because I think of myself as a good person. I know my mom is, and Peter was, the best of people. Why didn't God see it that way?

Two people have recently shared with me similar visions of God: God as a parent. And a parent can't prevent their child's pain; they can only be there when it happens. A parent supports a child through their agony. These people have said God is doing that for me right now. Life is fragile, and God can't help the breaks, only comfort me while picking up the pieces.

I'd like to get there one day because I do like these people's ideas of God. I do. I want to think none of this was God's fault or the will of God, that God isn't the ultimate controller. It paints God as more approachable, more part of me, and more like me. It erases the angry God, the scorekeeping God, the guilt-inducing God I kept in me for so long. And yet, I can't. Not right now. I can't embrace any version of God.

I am trying to get back to praying. My anger, confusion, and sadness are all preventing me. Right now, I am not sure I even believe in any version of God. Maybe it's good I have these strong feelings and endless questions. Perhaps they mean I still have some sort of belief in God. Possibly that part isn't dead in me after all; instead, it's in a coma. Or maybe, I still fear where my questioning, my anger, will fall on God's tally list.

Credit for Learning

The other night, I called the credit card company to remove Peter's name from the account. It was a difficult call. One of the first of many to change our joint accounts to singular. I have repeated Peter's story of his death so many times for family, friends, insurance companies, his work benefits companies, coworkers, and fill-in-the-blank, it's almost like I'm saying the Pledge of Allegiance when I repeat it. However, this time, it cut a bit deeper since it was the first time I removed him from my life.

I called the first credit company and requested to make Peter and my joint credit card mine alone. There was a pause, and then she replied with a very matter-of-fact response, "This is only Peter's account, not a joint one." Apparently, I was a carrier on the account. I was not a co-owner, which stunned me. I had no idea.

The representative transferred me to another department where I could open up a similar account. *Fine*, I thought, *I'll pick myself up from the ground, dust my disbelief off, and move ahead*. Another nice customer service person looked up my credit history. She told me it showed I didn't have a credit history, let alone a credit score. No, no. It's possible. I'm proof.

Not only did the joint credit card I thought I held with Peter not exist, but all of our utilities, and our two cars, were in Peter's name. Sure, the mortgage and the bank accounts were in both of our names, but evidently, nothing else. The excellent credit I thought that was ours was just Peter's. Score? Eight-hundred-something for Peter, zero for me.

At fifty-seven years old, I am starting all over again to build up my credit from scratch. Oh, I know it's going to be okay. My brilliant accountant friend, one of my best friends who talked me down when I exploded on the phone with her right after it happened, reassured me, as did my financial advisor. Still, at my age, building up credit is so stupid, so avoidable, and so harsh, with everything else going on in my life.

Starting from scratch with credit is humiliating, yet it's a bit metaphoric. It's reflective of my life right now. I am starting over—in so many ways. I am building a new me that I don't understand yet. My association with Peter is different now. I am not his wife; I am his widow. I am not his cohort. I am my own. I am not this woman dependent on her husband anymore. I am trying to find my independence. Maybe shedding Peter from my identity and finding comfort in my skin means shedding the old from my life. Perhaps this climb down the credit rabbit hole was a tap from Universe, or even Peter, to find my way, my new definition. It hurts like hell, but I think that's why they call it growing pains.

Anyone in a marriage or partnership should not assume all your financials are in order. Don't rely so heavily on the partner who handles finances because one day, he/she will die. No one lives forever. Most partners don't die together—something I always wanted, but you know, it just doesn't happen often. So get to know your finances and understand them and their consequences. Educate yourself, and if you don't understand, learn. No matter how boring you find it, learn. You can yawn later. Ask questions. Get answers. And for your sake, make sure you have your own credit card. If you think you're good with a joint one, like me, make sure it's actually a joint account. Get your name on most of your shared assets like cars and utilities. Have some of them in your name only. Share the wealth. Share the assets. Share the responsibility.

None of this was Peter's fault or my fault. It was both of our mistakes. I didn't pay attention to anything financial, and it bit me in my widowed ass. Peter, probably thinking he did the bills anyway, just took care of it, like he took care of everything in our lives. He took care of me, fully and completely and lovingly, but his generosity is yet another bite mark on my widowed ass. I know Peter didn't have a cruel intention or bone in his body to think, *Oh, let me screw with Betsy.* He couldn't have known he was going to die. Still, it was a mistake, pure and simple, made by both of us, two imperfect people, and I am angry at both Peter and me.

As flippant as this sounds, it is what it is. I can stay angry at Peter and me or forgive us both and move on. I have always had a hard time hanging onto anger. It never seemed to serve a purpose. The way I look at it is I can get angry, and there are times when I need to get angry, but then I need to confront, talk it over, and move on. Sometimes, I just move on without confrontation, especially when I see the silliness in a misunderstanding. For me to continue to beat myself up over this credit mistake will only knock me down further, and I don't know how much lower I can go. Holding anger toward Peter is just stupid. He can't even defend himself, although I would like to know what he was thinking. He was such a smart man. But I can't, and as I said, it was a mistake that I had an equal part in creating.

I have learned so much. I've learned more about myself, my capabilities, my rebounding techniques, and my self-reliance. I have learned more about finances and credit—both of which had me nodding off before, and maybe still, but are necessary in the grown-up world I didn't want to face before Peter's death. I'm slowly learning that I'm doing the best I know how to do, mistakes and all, present and past. And yeah, I'm a little proud of myself.

Impatience, Thy Name is Death

I've always been an impatient person. This revelation won't shock anyone who knows me. I'm not impatient with people, babies, or puppies. But I am impatient with situations like waiting in line, being in a traffic jam, rude people, and any general loss of control. Peter's death has made my impatience more frequent, and I am finding it harder to hide.

Recently, a web of confusion spun by insurance companies, a human resource department, the social security office, banks, and investment brokers caught me. I understand the hoops I have to jump through are not there because of kicks and giggles. Just like I know a truck doesn't decide to turn over in the middle of a highway to delay my travels and piss me off. I get it. All these companies and employees are doing is what they are supposed to do. In today's technological world, strict security is necessary. I should appreciate their diligence, and I do, but it doesn't stop my frustration living with this whole goddamn mess.

I am sure if I broke it down in a therapist's office, my frustration, my impatience, my frustration with my impatience, all come down to the loss of control I have in my life since Peter died. His sudden death is a giant, neon sign blinking over me as a constant example of how I couldn't stop any of this from happening. There was no purpose in his death, no sudden grab of a child's hand to prevent running in the streets. His death occurred because it did, without reason, without prevention from me. All my extreme irritation from the lack of control ignites my anxiety, or maybe my anxiety causes me to feel extreme irritation. I don't know. It's a chicken or the egg type question. I'll work through it, and until I get there, accepting impatience as part of me, part of my life now, is not going to happen. Not now. Not when the one thing I could not prevent, could not stop, could not even see as an eventuality, disrupted my life, perhaps forever—the death of my mister.

Peter was my calm through my raging storms, tantrums, complaints, and heavy sighs in uncontrollable situations. When I squirmed and objected to being stuck on the Eisenhower, he would ask me, "Do you have a plane to catch?" With every health scare, he countered my *what-if's* with *what-if-not's*. If someone cut me off in traffic and I put my hand on the horn to let that driver know how upset I was, Peter would smile and say, "Maybe his wife is having a baby." If someone stepped in front of me in the grocery line, Peter would chuckle and say, "They must be starving."

In the face of stress, Peter remained laid-back, unaffected by it. He reminded me to relax, with the constant question of, "Why are you worried or upset about something you can't do anything about?" Sometimes, it calmed me, and sometimes, it infuriated me because I wanted him to be as upset as I was. I don't have him anymore to temper the hurricane I'm living through now. He died, and so did the calm in my life.

It's not only the paperwork, the bouncing around on those ludicrous automated phone calls, the security questions, or even the waiting that are igniting my impatience, although they play a role. I don't even think it's my anxiety causing me to lash out at people who are just doing their jobs. It's the loss of control I feel from Peter's death, since Peter's death. It's the inability to start closing doors on some of this pain I hold with me every minute of every day. It's another break in my heart every time I retell the story that begins with, "My husband died." Mostly, it's not having him anymore to help me navigate these choppy, agonizing waves of life with his calming words. I have to do it alone, without my mister, my Peter.

Dog Days of Pain

These past forty-eight hours have been horrible. After climbing toward something close to okay, I have fallen to the ground in agony. It started when my daughter came home for the weekend. My son dropped by, and the three of us were together again. In a tiny glimpse of what once was, we told stories and laughed. They drank a few bottles of beer, and I had two glasses of wine. We were silly, and no tears came. No reminiscing of the past until it hurt. Not even a discussion of Peter's absence in our lives. It was a night of pure goofiness, which has always been a staple in our family. We pushed away any discussion on Peter's ashes at the funeral home, ready for pickup.

The next day started well enough. After wanting one for years (which friends and family can attest to), I rescued a dog only to return him the next morning because of my extremely uncomfortable allergic reaction. A dog bath and a human shower did not change anything. I was allergic to this dog—only the second dog I was ever allergic to, after years of growing up with dogs and having dogs in my life with Peter.

Returning the dog—and I did rename it, but I can't write it, as it would make it all the worse—was devastating. Devastation has appeared to rule my life since my husband died. In my old life, I would have had Peter for comfort or a *"told-you-so"* lecture (Peter didn't want another dog). I wanted, for once, a little sliver of happiness. Even a semblance of emotional normalcy would have fed my soul. I wanted easy after all the hard. I wanted a decision made without Peter to work, but I failed. Sure, I didn't know my body would react with hives and welts, but it was still, well, a failure. I know failure is inevitable in the pursuit of success. The lessons of failing without Peter carry much more unhappiness and insecurity, though. This failure crushed me, sent me tumbling backward. I slipped when I thought I was climbing out of the melancholy and deep grief.

The next day, I could no longer avoid the elephant in the room—Peter's ashes. I needed to get them. The funeral home didn't necessarily give me a specific deadline, but I needed to get them and get it done. With my daughter home, it seemed like the right timing. My stomach knotted so tightly that morning that it squeezed the sobs out of me. Peter's ashes "coming home," as someone called it, meant one more reckoning with the finality of his life. To say it was hard would be too soft.

Maybe I tried to fast-forward through the inevitable agony of collecting his ashes by getting a dog. Perhaps I thought the dog could be a distraction or offset some of my pain. Maybe the welts and hives were a sign from the Universe, God if She/He/They is still there, telling me there is no way to fast-forward through any of this. Feeling pain is inevitable, unable to be cured by a Band-Aid in form of a dog.

I returned the dog the next day. My daughter, sensing my devastation, told me that all we can do, all we are capable of doing right now, is getting through the day. And when we wake up in the morning, we can look back and say, "Well, at least we made it through yesterday." Getting through life, torturous one day after another, is the most demanding journey I have ever been on in my life.

Through the Storms

Peter and I drove through an ice storm once, during the part of the day when light surrenders to darkness. The bullets of chilled rain bounced off the roof of the car in a deafening beat. Frozen streaks of water clung to the windshield, not letting go even when the wipers tried to push them off. We reached areas where blankets of black ice lay before us. In our thirty-two years together, we had driven through many conditions, but this drive was the scariest.

Peter and I were driving home from somewhere. I don't remember where. We traveled a lot together. We took day trips to his hometown an hour and a half away, and five-hour drives to spend time with my daughter in college. In the past few years, we spent long weekends in surrounding states. He loved to drive, and I loved the lull of a moving car as I daydreamed about another one of my stories waiting for me to write. He wasn't a talker, and I learned to enjoy the quiet of a drive except for the music that sometimes blared through my headphones.

I said a mental rosary during this particular ice storm, hoping Mary would deliver us home safely. From time to time, I looked at Peter to tell him I was scared. He repeatedly assured me we were okay and that he had seen worse. Peter learned to drive on country roads in dangerous conditions. He often told stories of his adventures driving on roads never plowed of snow, or ditches calling cars into them. I often teased Peter with the same sarcastic question, if he also walked to school in six feet of snow, backward. He would smile, and I would laugh every time. This time, though, there was no back-and-forth. Peter's concentration was on the road blackened with ice, while I focused on the rosary's prayer order. Despite the wheel's occasional whip to correct a slide or a slow move across the frozen pavement, we eventually got home that night. When we did, there was an overwhelming sense of pride in me of being married to a superhero.

There were not many times in our relationship where I doubted Peter or his abilities. Most of the time, I felt we could and would make it through any storm, real or metaphoric, because of him. If I broke something, which I often did, I was confident Peter would fix it. When he faced numerous layoff worries during his almost thirty-eight years with the same company, he dodged those bullets with superhuman perfection. I never doubted he would be there for me through another one of my health scares. I felt secure in a crowd of unruly people with Peter by my side, assuring my safety. I knew all of this because he was my protector through everything. He always came home to me, safely, with a job, in good health, through a storm, until he didn't.

One of the things I grapple with during my sleepless nights since his death—and believe me, there have been too many—was the man I thought was invincible, died. Not only did he die, but he died in an accident, an accident where he took all the precautions in the world, including checking the weather radar, wearing head-to-toe protective motorcycle gear, and, knowing him, riding the speed limit. I thought how this man, who got us home in a violent ice storm, died in an accident on a clear, sunny day. Not only that, but he died before me: a woman who had cancer scares a few times in her life and had been in more fender benders than him. It was not fair, and it took away part of who he was to me.

There are so many losses I experienced because of the death of Peter, my chosen life-partner. I lost the smell of him, the taste of him, the feel of him, the look of him, the everydayness of him, the humor of him, the quietness of him, and I lost my protector through the storms of my life.

Anger

All my anger makes me bone-weary, and it doesn't surprise me. My heart found a home on my sleeve at birth, and deep emotions are my byproducts. I am angry by how these emotions control my time now since Peter died. I am angry that I can't help but wake up in tears, weep during the day, then sob out my loneliness at night. I don't have a handle on my sadness. I wish I could go away, take an extended vacation, and try to forget this all. I know a holiday won't make me forget any of this, and that pisses me off.

I'm also angry at being told how I should feel or "given permission" to feel. I didn't ask for it. Telling me I should be kind to myself, telling me I should do this or that to heal, even telling me it's okay only frustrates me. No one can possibly know the depths of the despair of another. Even more, I feel like no one can possibly know my pain. I'm angry for people thinking they do.

I'm angry about being told how strong I am. The fights with insurance companies and HR departments weaken me, so I wish people would let me be weak. Even the strongest warriors deflate in the agony of defeat, and I am facing my most significant losses ever. Let me feel my sufferings, my losses, and all that entails. Shut up about strength already. I don't always have it, and I never wanted it.

I'm angry at the drive-thru gal who tells me to have a nice day, the telemarketer who asks for Peter, and the couple that walks up and down the aisles of the grocery store with grasped hands. To the drive-thru girl, how can I have a nice day? I haven't had one of those in forever. To the telemarketer, no, you can't talk to my husband because see, he's dead and I will never speak to him again. To the couple over there holding hands, you two have what I will never have again. How dare people go on with their lives as if nothing happened! Don't they know my world stopped, and I can't stand to see others keep moving?

I am angry with people telling me they understand. Really? How? Unless your spouse, partner, or child died, I don't think you know my journey. Your friend's mother who just died is just not the same. The definition of yourself remains. Sure, you suffered a loss and are going through grief, but our pain and our losses are not the same. Quit trying to connect with me because I can't be connected to, not now, not yet.

I'm angry at people who tell me it'll all be alright and to give it time. How do they know? Do they have a crystal ball? And if so, why didn't they tell me what they saw before my husband died? I could have used it then. Hearing this from someone with a dead spouse is one thing. Hearing it from someone else does nothing for me. And yes, eventually, I will be alright. I have to be. There is no plan B, but just let me get there my way, at my pace.

I am so angry with myself, which is the most exhausting. I know the advice, encouragement, and stories come from a place of love and kindness. I believe in kindness. I've been surrounded by kindness so much in my life, especially since my husband died. As much as I struggle with the existence of God in all of this, sometimes, when I feel and see kindness, especially the type I've felt since Peter died, I think perhaps God exists. And yet, the possibility of this does not take away my anger, which is so exhausting.

I am not proud of myself. I hate that I have this anger and these thoughts right now. Unfortunately, or fortunately, I have a hard time sugarcoating my emotions. I feel every raw emotion, and sometimes, I will be unkind. So, to the people who see me with an angry sneer on my face when you wish me a good day, to those who talk about my strength, and to everyone who simply goes on with their lives, please do not take any of what I write here today personally. This is on me and where I'm at, and not on you and all your best intentions. I know kindness will one day return in me, but not while I am up on anger's stage.

Sick of This

I'm not feeling well today. My throat is sore, and my body aches. *"They"* say grief does that to you, knocks your body around, and leaves you feeling like crap. It doesn't help that I'm not eating properly. I am confident my recent diet of ice cream bars and bacon, foods I don't usually eat consistently, if at all—I am one of those weirdos who does not love bacon—are not on any food pyramid. Yet those are the foods I've been consuming most of the time; that is when I have an appetite, which isn't often.

Then there's the lack of sleep. I've always been a poor sleeper, the kind that rips off sheets and gets up every hour. I've been doing both since I can remember sleeping. I think part of it is because I have unsettling dreams. I remember all of them. (I've never wanted to pursue acting, maybe because I act so often during my dreams at night and acting in my waking life would be repetitive.) I don't talk in my sleep; at least I have not been told I converse in my slumber. But I do toss, turn, claw at sheets, and wake up. I'm a horrible sleeper. Now, in my grief, I find sleep is even more difficult and elusive.

Lately, I have a hard time just relaxing during the day. My mind, which is stuck on auto-play all the time, fast-forwards, skipping over the relaxing times. Since Peter died, it feels like there are ten million things I need to get done, or else that's what my anxiety tells me. I think that happens more when a spouse or partner dies suddenly. All the projects left undone, all the discussions for the future left unspoken, all the plans in a marriage left unplanned, and all the pleas for help in building tomorrow left unanswered, like a machine's cogged wheel with too many loose screws. I try to quiet my thoughts, and I succeed once in a great while, but then I look at a folder of bills sitting on a desk, or I get an email from an insurance company, or something comes in the mail, and my mind's gears start moving again and won't stop, almost like the gears were stripped.

And, of course, there's the crying. I am an emotional crier. I don't cry from pain very often. I have a high tolerance for it—being klutzy at an early age toughened me up. But emotional pain? Um, yeah.

During our thirty-two years together, Peter grew so accustomed to my tears, he kind of ignored them. I don't mean that cruelly; rather, he treated my tears like I had a tic. I understood. Emotional tears were as much a part of me as blowing my nose during a cold. Still, since Peter died, I have cried more than I have ever cried in my life. There has not been one single day since he died when I have gone without crying. Not just tears slipping down my cheeks, but sobbing, ugly cries. The crying where your gut tightens, your heart hurts, and your throat convulses. My cries are full of anguish and so deep, any hope for some resemblance of joy disappears with each dry heave after the tears. That is exhausting. And it does not do the body any good.

I hope this all makes sense. Maybe it doesn't because I feel crappy and am scattered, more than usual. No one has to tell me grief caused this. I don't have to hear my sore throat and body aches are from grieving. It's obvious. Most days, I work toward a time of moving on. Today, I fear there is no actual recovery from all that is gone, just figuring out how to adjust. But I know I feel this fear today, because today, I am sick.

Come out, Come Out, Wherever I Am

Apparently, the world is still going on. Other things are happening in our country, in our world, while I'm in mourning. I can't tell you about all the happenings, but I know I've at least read some dribs and drabs of news. Since Peter's death, I have cut myself off from the world. Yes, I have gone out a few times, and people have come to see me. I have received emails, phone calls, messages, and texts. Yes, I've read excerpts from social media. Most of the time though, my world has been about me.

When I'd first talk to a friend or family after Peter died, the entire conversation revolved around me and my emotions. In the beginning, I didn't care. I didn't have the compassion to ask about anyone else's life. My heart was too broken, too numb, and my concern or curiosity didn't exist. I'm getting better. I think. Not a lot better, but somewhat. Maybe it's progress. Perhaps I'm trying to do better due to fear of losing important people in my life. Insecurity rears its ugly head yet again. Perhaps I'm trying to grab onto some normalcy. Or maybe I'm tired and bored, bored and tired, of myself and my emotions.

I don't want to close off the world and all the people in it. But for now, it seems to be my coping mechanism. My usual compassion has taken the back seat to deal with myself and Peter's death. This sucks because it's not who

I am, who I was. I'm not even sure of who I am anymore. I bet my definition of myself will keep alternating until I learn to adjust to life without him. Oh, I'll never be who I once was. All I can hope is to emerge a similarly compassionate person with some fire left in her.

See, that's the other thing missing from me: any spark for social justice. Before Peter's death, I was someone who not just spoke out, but *shouted* out against injustices. Words would never stay jailed in my mouth or my writing when it came to racism, anti-LGBTQ+ rhetoric, xenophobia, misogyny, sex trafficking, and on and on and on. Now? I have no shout left in me.

My first meeting with Peter was at a volleyball game where we struck up a conversation about Chicago politics. We were both sitting o the sidelines, waiting for our rotation back in. Being a political science major, with an emphasis on Chicago politics, and a groupie of the famous Chicago newspaper political columnist of the '70s, Mike Royko, I relished these types of conversations. Peter and my first conversation had me thinking *I want this man in my life longer than this.* I thought, *maybe there's something to this shy boy with the nice butt.*

As our relationship grew, so did the recognition of the similarities of our beings. We held the same indignation for the inequitable treatment of people. When we married and had children, we chose to live in a town with diversity, an essential need for our children. We taught our children the wrongs of any prejudice. We accepted people for their personhood. I had so many years of Peter having my back while expressing my feelings on equity and inclusion.

What started as my spark with him ignited into a lifelong, well *his* lifelong, relationship.

I know there are so many things going on globally, and I missed opportunities these past few weeks to lift my voice in protest. My fire is gone, put out by Peter's death. The person who was my soft place to land after an ugly rally or a heated exchange will never be in my life again. With his exit, this fire inside me is hiding, and right now, I don't have the energy to find it.

A Sail of a Story

There is a story I like to tell. A story full of twists, turns, oddities, and coincidences if you believe in them. It's a story of a Father's Day card, a painting, the days before Peter's death, and how I hope this tale will always remain part of Peter's story. It's a long one, but one I want to tell it now, while it's still fresh in my memory. Stories become convoluted, or pieces are left out or blown up like a fisherman's tale. But what I will share next is what I hope to always remember, the way it was when Peter was alive.

I have to start back a few years ago, on Mother's Day 2017, when my adored niece died. Racheal was Peter's godchild, the only daughter of Peter's twin sister, Trisha. Racheal had one of those spirits I wanted to be around. She drew me in with her soft humor, her kind words, how fully engaged she became when she listened, and an indescribable beauty radiating from within. She had a way of listening as if you were the only one in the room. I admired Racheal's fondness for people in her life, most notably her grandmother and brothers.

Racheal and her Uncle Pete got along very well. There was a connection between them, perhaps formed as an extension from a twin's bond. Their relationship of godfather to goddaughter was strong. When she died, devastation hit us both, but especially Peter. I experienced

Peter's sadness from the death of his mother and father. This sadness came from a different place, a place of questioning the death of someone so young.

Fast forward to Peter's last Father's Day. My daughter, who lives five hours away, had to work that weekend and wasn't going to be able to come home to celebrate. Since she knew she wouldn't see him on the day, she mailed Peter a card that started an unlikely stream of events.

The card came the day before Father's Day. It showed a scene of sailing on its cover, one of Peter's loves. (He was a member of a sailing club. He sailed every summer on Lake Michigan and even sailed the Virgin Island once. He always did what he loved without fear or regret.) The picture on the card captivated Peter. He stared at it for a long time before reading my daughter's message on the inside. When Peter turned the card over, he saw the name of the artist. The artist's name was Rachel Parker—the same first name, but with a different spelling, and last name as Racheal, his niece. This reveal touched Peter, maybe more than any gift my daughter could have given him.

Peter searched the internet and found the artist's name. He sent the artist a message and asked to purchase the artwork on his Father's Day card. Peter explained the card's story and the connection to his niece.

The artist informed Peter the painting he referred to was one of a few sail scenes she painted. Her paintings were mainly of animals like cats, dogs, and horses, and of landscapes. The painting Peter was referring to, the one on the card, hung in her house, and she was not looking to sell it. However, after hearing Peter's story, the artist agreed. She set a price, and without consulting me, something he never did on big purchases, Peter sent her a check. The artist took it off her wall and mailed it to Peter. Two days before Peter died, on an early Saturday afternoon, the painting arrived. I was visiting my mom and not home for the reveal. Our neighbors and friends, Dave and Lisa, were outside working. Lisa swept the inside of the garage while Dave worked on his boat. Peter walked up to Dave and told him the story of the painting and that it had arrived. After telling the story, Peter repeated a few times: "What do you think it means? It has to mean something. It has to." Dave told me later that Peter appeared unlike himself when he told the story—distant, almost like Peter was in a trance. For Peter to even question the painting's meaning was odd. He didn't question. He just lived.

After Peter finished telling his story to Dave and asking his questions, Lisa joined them. Peter repeated the story to her and asked the same questions. Lisa confirmed Dave's feelings. According to Lisa, as he told the story, Peter looked different, spoke different, and everything about the conversation was unsettling, different.

After he concluded the story to Lisa, Peter asked them both to come over to look at the painting. The three of them came into my house to look at it. Peter, again, repeated, "What does this mean? What do you think it means? It has to mean something, right?" Lisa and Dave reiterated even during this conversation in my home, as he stared at the painting, Peter was definitely "not himself."

When I pulled into the driveway that day, Peter was mowing the lawn. He stopped the mower, and with a big grin on his face came trotting over to me. He grabbed my hand and said, "Come in the house. I have to show you something." I already had an idea the painting arrived.

I looked at the painting propped up against our couch and glanced at Peter as he beamed at it—I mean, *beamed*. Peter was never a *"whoo-hoo, look what I bought"* type of guy. He never grew excited about too much, let alone purchases and gifts. After opening a gift on Christmas or his birthday, he would always respond, "Oh, this is nice," with words never projecting any kind of excitement. So with this painting, his animation startled me.

We hung the painting on the part of the wall that does not get much viewing. We agreed to eventually change its location once we had time to rework all the other pictures hanging on our walls. And that's where it stayed, without any more discussion, without further thought.

I am a believer in signs, in more profound meanings. After everything unfolded as it did, I wonder if Racheal reached out to Peter from beyond. Lisa thinks the painting was Racheal's way of telling Peter she was at peace. Perhaps. Maybe Peter did feel a sense of calm from knowing Racheal went gently into the night. But what I think, what I truly believe, is that the painting and the story behind it were our wonderful, loving niece's way of telling Peter she would see him soon. And she did. Two days after the painting arrived, Peter was killed.

I emailed the artist to give her closure to this story. As a writer, I enjoy people's responses to my creations. In my email, I wrote how four weeks later, her painting hangs in our, my, living room. I told her I chose new furniture and

accessories based on the colors in the painting. I explained
to her how I moved the image, and now it is the focal
point of the room, hanging over my head, in the place
where I write every day.

The painting will be mine for as long as I live. I
hope after I am gone, it will be handed down to future
generations. Not because of its beauty, although there is
that, but because of its story. It is Peter's story, a father's
story, a grandfather's story, a great-grandfather's story, or
perhaps an uncle's or great uncle's story. Whoever ends up
with it one hundred years from now, they will have a part
of Peter's story, a part I wanted to write down.

Painting © Rachel Parker, https://www.rachelsstudio.com/

A Painful Question

Is there a good way to die? To die with dignity is a good way. At least they said so in the old war movies I watched with my father. To *"die at peace"* has been said repeatedly for years as comfort to the survivors. To *"die without pain"* is another phrase doctors use to give solace to a family. To *"die at home"* is many people's wish. And to die *"surrounded by loved ones"* brings a particular joy to the living.

I've been thinking about this lately as I try to put together, piece by broken piece, what happened the afternoon Peter died. I am trying to fit together what I've read, what I've heard, and what I know for sure. The certainty is small, other than he died, and I don't have any official reports yet to tell me exact details. So I am stuck playing some kind of sleuth figuring out a killing in a macabre mystery book I want to either put down or finish, and I can't do either.

Unexpected deaths like Peter's take a little longer to get information on, and because of that, to grieve. I know about long, drawn-out illnesses. My father was sick all my life. He was in and out of hospitals with strokes, heart attacks, blockages, and more strokes. Eventually, his heart pumped too slowly and shut down the rest of his organs. It was not a good way to live a life—in pain, uncertainty, and hospital rooms. He made the best out of the life handed to him, something I admired greatly in him.

I said many goodbyes to my father, as death or life tricked my family often. These goodbyes eased my mind and my heart when he finally did die. I knew my father and I told each other, "I love you," said the things we needed to say, and in the end, I felt there were no words left unspoken between us.

Peter's death was different. It was instant. It was startling. It was a life snuffed out in minutes. There was no preparation for me, no goodbyes, too many words left unspoken between us, and questions never fully answered. Unfulfilled dreams for us, for him, for me, died with him. Confusion about our finances and financial stability clouded my brain. Decisions we made as a team, suddenly, all so suddenly, became a solo act. A final goodbye would never be, thus leaving me in a macabre state of flux.

I think about the night Peter died. I think about the words of the doctor: "*Your husband died instantly and in no pain.*" It meant nothing to me then. Sure, I repeated the words for family and friends, but I never really heard them; I never really felt them. All I heard and felt that night and the days that followed were the words, "*We did all we could,*" a final declaration of surrender. The rest was static to my ears. Peter's pain level didn't matter. All that mattered to me was that when Pater was taken by death, half of me died with him, and I began to mourn us both.

I don't know what a good way to die would look like to anyone. Maybe it comes down to what's best for the person dying versus what's best for the survivor. I don't know if it is better for the survivor to say goodbye to a loved one, even if it means the loved one is in pain. Or if it is better for the one dying to leave this world abruptly and without any last words to the survivors, but with little or no pain. The question of betterment between the way someone dies and what remains comes down to who gets the pain: the victim, or the survivor? Is this all a transference of pain? I don't know these answers. I don't think there are any.

In my best of days, I want to know Peter died without pain. I want to think his way was a good way to die, probably the best. On my worst, my most selfish days, I want to take it back because I think, *but I don't like the pain.* On most days, I sit and ponder the best way to die and for whom. In the end, I suppose it doesn't matter. The results are the same. Death always leaves someone in pain.

Masking with a Cape

Who Am I? That was the question I addressed once for a Christian organization I belonged to when I was eighteen. A committee chose me to give this talk to older teens and young adults. I fit the criteria because I was in the organization for a year and served on other, less noticeable committees like dinner prep and clean up.

In my speech, *Who Am I*, I spoke about finding myself as I transitioned from high school into college, seeking my independence. In one part of my speech, I talked about the different masks I wore to fit in. I told a story of how I, the ordinarily obedient high schooler, was now smoking in the back of Chicago city buses and cutting my college classes. I explained the confusion in all of this and my attempts to find myself while putting on different masks. I described the different masks I wore. One for my parents and family, another for the new friends I made, another for professors, another for my coworkers, and I saved my real face for the people who knew me best. At the end of the speech, I played the song about connecting to rainbows, and it was all groovy.

I thought about my speech and my eighteen-year-old self yesterday because the young me has become relatable again. No, I don't smoke anymore or ride CTA buses, and college is distant in my life's rearview mirror. But, like those days, since Peter died, I am struggling to find out who I am. Instead of masks, though, I wear a Super Widow cape and feel like a fraud.

I am not always who I project myself to be lately. Sometimes, I crack one-liners when I don't feel humorous. Or I pretend to listen to some people's stories while my mind wanders onto yet another thought of Peter. Sometimes, I push myself to tell others that yes I do see the gifts in my life, when all I want to do is revel in my bitterness. I say I don't need anything even though I do but can't seem to formulate what I need. I respond quickly with a, "I'm okay," like a twitch, when I am a miserable mess. I go through my days, hoping to put one foot in front of the other, and I feel as if I am on this insane hamster wheel of grief going nowhere.

Lately, I've been putting on a persona of someone who has it all together, hiding the crumbling person inside. I try to show excitement, or at least interest, because I don't want anyone to grow tired of me or see me as someone who can only talk about grief for her dead husband.

It's not always about my insecurities. Sometimes, I think faking it means making it, and I genuinely want to get back to my happy point before Peter died. I wish to be full of humor again and enjoy people's stories. I want to go back to when I was articulate, better than okay, and had a pep in most of the steps I took. I miss that person, that whole person, and not the person with half of her missing with no idea who she will become. The fear of all of this scares me, so I pretend sometimes. I pretend the personas and the emotions I don't feel.

Someone once told me, when you bury your feelings, you're burying them alive, and they will rise again in you. That someone was right. What you bury does sprout. With every ingenuine emotion I project, the pit in my stomach grows, and I struggle to keep it together. I let go of all I keep bottled up during the day with the release of tears in the dark loneliness of night. I know I have to make it through another day, which means being a fraud, if just for a few moments. I know I can't go around crying all the time or in utter sadness. That would only paralyze me more, stop me from getting through the day. And getting through the day is my only goal right now.

Others have told me to be kinder to myself, gentler to my progress and feelings. Kindness doesn't come easy in the hatred of my life. I have been told to do what it takes to get through the day, even if the phony cape I wear drags me down with pretending to be someone I am not. I question what is heavier, though, the cape or the truth of the weakness inside of me. In time, I know that through therapy and gaining more strength, I will take off the cape and just be me, broken me. It has to be alright, as it's the best I can do or be for now. Yet, *knowing* and *doing* live in two separate families. The work on blending them has not begun for me yet.

Who Am I? remains a great question, one I have no answer for, and, I fear, won't have for an awfully long time. And so, I have replaced the masks I wore at eighteen with the widow's cape I now wear forty years later.

Come Out From the Rain

Lately, I've been feeling like I'm standing in a thunderstorm with a broken ankle. I can't move without discomfort, so I put my hands over my head to try to deflect all that keeps coming down on me. Some things, like gentle showers, are more of a nuisance than anything else. Other things, like hail and pelts of rains, hurt when they make contact. No matter how hard I try, the rain keeps pouring down. I know I have to move, but every time I take a step, my busted ankle shoots pain up my leg. And so I stand there, fighting with the falling rain, making pained movements, crying out in agony and frustration.

There are so many things pouring down on me, things I need to get done, since Peter died. Things like yard work with growing weeds and neglected edging. The stuff, Peter's stuff, cluttering up the house in messy disorganization. Other things Peter handled, like insurances, pension, car maintenance, and bills, are teasing with deadlines. Essentials like groceries (or lack thereof), garbage days, and on and on, calling out their need for attention. I feel each pelt of daily life harder now because my partner of thirty-two years is not with me to shelter me from them.

My friend Laura told me one of the many reasons why a spousal death is so different than any other death is the remaining spouse is left doing the work of two. Or, in my case, doing the work of Peter, which was everything I never did before. It's overwhelming and frustrating. I feel like ignoring it all, but I know I can't. And I'm doing all of this with a broken heart. It all hurts like hell.

My children have been godsends in their support of me. They've taken over the bills until I can get my footing, as well as the maintenance of my car since I have no clue about those objects on four wheels. Friends and family have offered to help. Many are "there" to help me deflect or grab hold of some of these things Life is throwing at me. I just have to continue to ask.

I have a hard time asking for help, and I don't know why. I mean, all someone can say is yes or no. I don't know what I fear. That's a lie. I do. I fear the rejection of a no. I am a sensitive person (shocker!), even more so in my grief right now. I have pride and ego that tell me I can do it alone. I mean, isn't that what so many of us women do most of our lives? Try to go it alone? I can't ask for help because my control issues prevent me from giving up any power to someone else.

I am also struggling with words to articulate what I want since my mind is so jumbled in grief. I'm good with the written word, but lately, my verbal skills suck. Besides, how do I ask some to people to perform the Heimlich when I'm choking? I wish they would just do which I know can be unrealistic, but my exhaustion tells me such an expectation is reasonable. And honestly, some things are intimate and allow people too much of a glimpse into me and my life with Peter. After all, Peter was half of me, and I'd be opening up the half now. So, I don't ask for help.

Despite all my reluctance, I know I have to start asking. The people I keep company with will help me, no doubt. And if they don't, there will be a good reason or an open-ended invitation to ask again. I need to receive a yes and a no with equal acceptance. Peter once told me when you request a favor, receive a no as you would a yes; otherwise, you are telling, not asking. Beautiful and wise, right?

When I get bombarded with the raindrops of all I have to take care of now that Peter is gone, I am sure there will be someone in my life lending a hand. My life is full of good people. I need to ignore my unwillingness to ask and just do. Otherwise, my life's burdens, the burdens left when Peter left this world, will continue to fall on me for a very, very long time.

My Mom and Her Baby

I came in through the front doors like I usually do, and I saw her in the common area, sitting in her wheelchair, parked by the unlit fireplace on the hot summer day. She stared out the window, then darted her eyes around the room as if searching for something. When they landed on me, her face dropped, and she began to cry. Her arms shot out to me as she sobbed, "Oh, my baby. My baby. You're here."

I scurried over to her, dropped my purse, fell into her arms, and wept. "I hurt, Mom," I cried. "I hurt so much." She cooed into my ear over and over, "My baby. My poor, poor baby." We stayed like that for a few minutes—me, knocking on sixty's door, hugging my mother like I was ten again, and she, in one of her rare lucid moments, comforting me like the baby she was calling me.

After Peter's death, I needed my mother. No matter my age, I needed my mom. But the mother I once knew was now pretty well gone. The mother who always introduced me as "my baby," since I am the youngest of her seven children, was the mom I needed. I knew *that* mom was gone. I knew because I've mourned the loss of her a few times now. So, if all I saw was this shell of what my mother used to be, it would destroy me, and I was already shaky at best.

My mother resides behind a sheet of senility, only peeking out for a few moments at a time now. Even during her lucid moments, the nonsensical and the absurd show up. Seeing her would mean I would have to remind her Peter was dead, or worse, pretend he wasn't. Out of respect for her and her feelings of frustration, I try not to correct her, and pretending would be too hard.

My mother told me a week before Peter died, in her confused speech, she wanted to die. She listed all her loved ones who have already died, then talked about how much she longed to see them again, in heaven. She remains on Earth, a shell of who she once was, and it causes anger and frustration in me. A cruel and painful slap was delivered to me when death ignored my mother's pleas to leave and instead took my husband. A question I repeated aloud to anyone listening was: how can a person who wants to die, with a life fully lived and in poor health, remain, while my husband, who had years left, who had not yet grown old with my children or with me, was taken? How?

For these reasons and, in need of self-preservation, I hadn't visited my mother since Peter died. I know these are selfish reasons, maybe even unkind. Yet, I felt a need to protect my crumbling heart from falling apart completely, and the only way to do this was by avoidance. And then, well, I did finally go and see her.

Maybe I decided to visit because I'm in a better place now, and my anger and expectations are lower. Maybe I wanted to rip the fucking Band-Aid off, because never seeing my mom again could not be an option. Maybe I wanted my mom in any form. Whatever the reason, I got into my car, headed out on the first of three expressways that got me there, and went to spend some of my morning with my mom. And in one beautiful gift of a morning, my mom returned. Yesterday, my mom was lucid as she held me. She called me what I needed to be—her baby. What's more, she treated me like I was her baby. She didn't tell me it was going to be alright. Being a widow herself, she couldn't lie to me. Instead, she held me and soothed me and treated me like her child, a child she knew and remembered. After all the responsibilities I faced lately and the strength I've mustered to put one foot in front of another, it felt good and right to be comforted and protected in the arms of my mother.

We sat for the rest of the visit, holding hands. My mother continuously squeezed mine, telling me how much she missed me, worried about me, wished she could have been there for me. My mother apologetically explained why she couldn't be at Peter's memorial service, which of course, I already understood, but she nevertheless felt the need to say. She told me I was her "mushka"—an endearing Polish nickname she and my dad called me—and she wished I didn't have to go through this because I didn't deserve it, and neither did my kids. She told stories of Peter. Some of them were true, and some were only true to her. It didn't matter. What mattered was they were stories from a place of deep love for Peter, whom she loved like a son.

I left her with a promise to return to my once per week routine, which pleased her. Walking to my car, I knew my future visits would most likely not go this well. Still, I held onto what I had in *this* visit, my first one since Peter died. Perhaps my daughter was right. Perhaps yesterday morning was the reason my mother is still living, so she could come back to me, her baby, when I needed her the most.

Better Than

That is what I have strived to achieve in my life— better than. My writing should be better than a few years ago. My life lessons continue to teach me better than I knew yesterday. My work assignments are better than the last one in my learning curve. And my house decoration decisions make my home better than before. To me, better than is a way to measure the past and present to improve. I try to do better than in all aspects of my life, which is even more evident in widowhood.

Every day since Peter died, I want to do better than a period before. I want to feel better than I did the week or the day before, the hour earlier, whether that means having less fall-apart moments or crying just a little less. I want to be better than in looking for the gifts inside this nightmare because, in these searches, I will find more of myself. I want to be better than my patience for people when I retell Peter's stories, whether with neighbors, coworkers, friends, family members, or customer service. I want to be better than holding it together when I need to release it, when I should. I want to be better than I have been living my life since this horror show started. I don't have to be happy in it—that won't happen for a long time—but being able to walk through it better than before and less scared.

Being better than does not mean perfection. There is no such thing as perfection, and even if there were, I wouldn't have it in me to attempt it. Besides, I can't put that pressure on myself. No, better than right now means trying to get closer to okay. I have to face the reality of my widowhood, my life without a partner, the stress, the falls, the everydayness better than each day. I have to be better than saying fuck you to life, fuck you. I have to include with my profanity that I'm going to make it and mean it. I need to see and embrace these better-than's, even with insecurities or *yeah, but*'s, to move closer to being okay.

Looking back to how I was the week Peter died, the weeks following his death, and even yesterday, I have done better than. I am still standing. Not only standing but walking and talking. Sure, I cry and scream and swear, but I keep going. I keep standing. Once in a while, I laugh, and sometimes, I actually feel like laughing.

The death of a spouse is different than any other death. There's no walking away from any of this. I can't go home. I *am* home, a home I shared with my spouse, with memories packed in like pungent sardines. I don't have the support of a spouse to get me through this. He's dead. I have constants like paperwork and people and stuff, his stuff, surrounding me shouting, *"He's not coming back!"* I have no escape from any of this. It's just me. Sure there is a wonderful group of people in my life, but really, just me. I need to get better than to survive this horror of a time that, for the most part, I can't believe is mine. So, yeah, I do look at the better-than's as victories, small or big. They are my survival tool right now.

Last night, I was with two of my besties—sisters, really—and I told them I was there once in the darker place, and now I'm here, in a lighter one. I still hurt every day. I still wake up thinking, *Oh shit, Peter's dead.* I still have a hard time moving. I still am scared about my future. I still have half of me ripped away, feeling exposed. I'm still trying to figure it all out. And yet, here, right now, I am doing better than back there, behind me. Up ahead, there may be even better than waiting. But I can't worry about what's up there. All I can hold onto is what I see now, the better than yesterday.

Coming Down from the Tower

Six years ago, I spent a weekend alone at a bed-and-breakfast in Saugatuck, Michigan, a tiny town I escaped to, alone, without kids or Peter. Three of my friends gave me a weekend away to write for my birthday. It was a comfortable B & B, the owner was friendly, and it was close to town for exploring during my breaks from writing. On the first exciting night of being on my own without interruption, the excitement brought peace, contentment, and love toward my friends who gave me the gift.

The second day, those feelings waned, replaced with an odd sensation. I felt like I was on an observation deck of a tall tower, watching someone else's life unfold below. Being a mom and wife, I never went anywhere by myself for long. Sometimes, I had getaways with friends, but never on my own, at least not since the single days of my twenties. So, the aloneness was an odd feeling and all so surreal to me. I'm not sure I'm describing it well enough, this feeling of being removed from my own experience, but it's the best I can put into words from outside myself.

Fast forward six years, and my life is now that of a widow. I am living a life without my person, and it has been unreal. I got over the shock of Peter's death as time has passed. mark hit. I finally grasped that Peter had, in fact, died, and I moved past the sense of living outside myself as I held the same feeling of being in my observation tower, in disbelief and sadness. I tried to reconcile it all.

Now, I am moving off the observation deck of the tower and toward the reality of my life. The descending process brings with it a longing for Peter so intense, it pulls my emotions from places I held shut. The acknowledgement of my life without Peter creates a new, stronger desire to have him back. I am not looking at my life. I am in my life, a life without Peter. This certainty brings in new forms of agony and pain and longing as I descend. New emotions rush through me like a toxic injection in my veins. With each little step away from detachment, it hurts—so much so, I wish with every part of me, I could climb back up the tower to my observation perch. Too late. The steps back there are greased with reality.

Because I Have To

When I was a teenager, I once asked my mother how she did it. How did she work full-time, take care of a sick husband, raise seven kids, and go on with life? Her answer was brief. She answered, "I do it because I have to." For my sixteen-year-old self, looking at life full of opportunities and choices, this didn't make sense. "You don't have to do anything you don't want to do," my then-naive self said. As I got older, married, and had kids of my own, it made more sense. Life sometimes strips you of choices. And now, as a widow, with the life of the man I chose taken from me, I get it. I get the "because I have to" part of life.

This week, I have finally received some of Peter's benefits. It feels as if a particular insurance company loves to dole out requirements in pieces. I almost picture Boris and Natasha-type characters, laughing when I hang up with them because they know I am missing something important. When I call back to inquire about why I had not received something yet, I feel they were holding down a chuckle as they responded, "Oh, forgot to tell you, you need this too." I'm kidding, of course. I don't *really* think the customer service people are out to screw me. Although . . . never mind. After so many phone calls, so many discussions with lawyers, friends, my kids, and a financial advisor, I am finally starting to get my husband's death benefits. A victory for me since he was the provider of the salary bread. Yay me. I worked my way through the web of bureaucratic confusion. And I did it because I had to. The other night, I read an email from my friend Laura, a sister in widowhood, telling me she had to change her house's air filters, one of the things I never even thought of doing. I texted my neighbor friend, asking about air filters. He offered to come down and check for me, which was kind and generous and so like him. But I decided to figure it out on my own. I did. I changed the house's air filter. I didn't have to do this, but I wanted to because I'm stubborn, and I needed to know, and the only way I could learn was by doing it—a little bit of a victory there.

I also had mice in my house last week. I believe they came from an overgrown yard next door or my unattended vegetable garden I no longer want nor need. The garden was Peter's, not mine, and I can't bring myself to maintain it. No matter. The mice came into my house. So, guess what I do? Besides calling an exterminator—I can only catch and release so many times—I called the yard's property owner next door to me. I explained the situation to the owner, even adding in Peter's death. She honestly did not know the yard got that bad, and I believe her. I have no reason not to. They were also once neighbors of ours, good, kind neighbors. When I told her Peter died, she cried. She thought Peter was one of the kindest people she ever has known. I cried too and blubbered out, "You're right; he was." Three hours later, the grass was mowed, the yard weeded, and extra garbage was thrown out from the property. I need to thank her. I have washed and cleaned out all my cabinets. Thanks to everything I did, including weeding the garden and calling an exterminator, the mice are gone. And, well, I did it because I had to. I mean, I can't be living with mice. Although, some of them were darling little buggers.

Yesterday, I arranged for a charity to take Peter's car. It's a 2003 SUV, with plenty of miles on it, and it leaks oil. The oil needs to be added to the engine every thousand miles. I didn't want to take care of two cars, and the charity is one of my favorite organizations and was also one of Peter's favorites. They do a lot for kids, especially older kids and teens at risk of being in trouble with the law. This decision was a slam dunk; only I had to put oil in it. So, I popped the hood and stared at the engine for a long time, as if it were an abstract painting. It took me a while to figure out what cap I needed to take off which part and fill. When I decided to take the plunge into oil adding, I took a deep breath, said a prayer to Peter, and poured. For a few minutes, I was a mechanic. Me! A person who can't tell the difference between a Honda and a Toyota sedan. I managed to do it because I had to.

I have faced many more situations I just had to—a broken lawnmower, weeds popping up everywhere, overgrown bushes, unfilled paperwork, unclosed accounts, and on and on. And on—it's a long list. Having to do these things has been as scary as the hell I'm living in since Peter died. It's been lonely. I am frustrated and angry while my blood pressure rises and my heart races. My appetite has left me, and my sleep is disturbed. It's hard for me to face all of this head-on by myself while grieving. But I do face it, head-on and myself.

I am proud of my victories, each one of them. I don't rejoice too long because I know another battle will be rising soon. But I'll fight again because I have to fight. My mother taught me so much, but this lesson may be one of her greatest—you do what you have to do. I've had to do a lot since Peter died. And somehow, I do it.

A Little Less at Book Club

In the weeks following Peter's death, all my thoughts, words, and feelings were about him. I couldn't hold a conversation without launching into monologues about everything Peter—my emotions, my love for him, my shock, memories, accolades, and everything. Every waking moment was about Peter, in one form or another. I suppose that's a normal stage, but to be honest, I kind of bored myself.

Last night I went to my neighborhood's book club with ladies who are lovely human beings. The "book" part of the club is a very loose term, as it seems we never really discuss the book. We spend more time catching up, talking about our kids, lives, ambitions, jobs, husbands, and ourselves than the actual book. We are a close-knit bunch—a bunch who came running when Peter died, providing me with food, comfort, and even a bonfire in his name. And last night, I felt like I let go of a little part of Peter, if only the tip of his pinky.

I've been working up to this. I find myself asking my friends questions about themselves more often. I'm laughing a bit more. My thoughts about Peter are still there constantly, but I have added normal thoughts to them. I still vomit up Peter stories or stories connecting to him, though not as often. Too often for some, maybe, yet I know it's less, and I don't know how I feel about it.

Yesterday I struggled to decide whether or not to go to book club. I had read the book before Peter's death, and I remembered bits and pieces. Widow fog erased most of it. As much as I love these women, and I do, very much, I didn't want to spend the night perhaps answering questions about Peter or excessively talking about him. I had a day full of Peter. I spent the day in unfinished Peter paperwork, with the final steps to release his car and final paperwork to be released into my name, and my name only. I spent the day in thoughts, solo rumination of him, and of course, crying about the absence of him. Escaping into a reality show of someone else's life, real or put on, felt like something to ease my Peter-filled mind. I didn't want to go to book club until I did.

I am glad I did. The night turned out fine. I reached the 'okay' mark. Yes, I did answer questions about Peter, and I did talk about him a lot, like *a lot*, and I'm so glad these women love me enough to let me do just that. And I cried some. But honestly, it was less than the weeks right after he died, even if the women who were there may not have thought so. Actual stories were going on, too. Stories I engaged in, asked questions about before I drifted off to thoughts of Peter.

Toward the end of my evening, one of the ladies talked about a new computer job she landed that sounded so cool, and I thought, *Oh, I have to tell Peter,* since computers were his profession. I got excited about this idea as fast as it devastated me when I realized there was no Peter anymore. An emptiness spread through me like a fever, and it didn't leave. It's always those small things that fill so much of me. Eventually, I left, jackrabbiting it out of there at the first opportunity. When I got home, I went to bed like I often do to avoid feeling anything more. And now, in the morning, I am okay. I am okay, and I am okay with the progress made by going out and not making *everything* about Peter. I made a lot about him, but not everything. 'Not everything' is progress.

What do all these things mean: the changing of names on paperwork, taking away his car, and cutting back on making it all about Peter? I guess it's a part of the progression of grief. It scares me, though. When I was back "there" in grief, I held onto Peter. When I'm "here," my grip loosens. When I reflect on "up there," I wonder how much more I will have let go of him. All the tangibles are slowly fading, and what is left are my words and remembrances. My brain is slowly storing memories, and they are less a part of my new world.

I need to let go of most eventually, to grasp onto something else like life as it is now. I know this because life can end with a snap of a finger. It is a special gift I need to unwrap every day and use. I also know this because I cannot become my new self without moving toward my different definition. Of all people, Peter would never have wanted me to make my life about him after he was gone. To move on, even with baby steps, is hard. It's scary as hell. It almost feels like a betrayal to Peter and his memory. But it's what I know I have to do. So, I start small with name changes, car donations, and "book" club.

Weekends

I felt like I was getting there—the place where I started to accept my new normal with a little less sadness, grief, or anger. While they stuck around, I didn't feel as paralyzed by it all. I even saw some small victories. I thought I was on my climb toward my new norm. I knew I had a way to go, but I was at least climbing. And then the weekend hit. It hit like the weekend before, the weekend before that, and I'm sure the weekends ahead. It hit hard and knocked me off my footing, causing me to plummet back down to when I first knew of his death—into the bowels of despair, the bowels of widowhood.

Among the many hard parts of widowhood—sadness, grief, longing, finances, paperwork, insecurities, and new definition—the hardest of them all is the intense loneliness. Loneliness brings with it a feeling of isolation and abandonment. It's not from a lack of friends or companionship; instead, it's from the lack of Peter and his intimacy. My longing for my husband is so strong, it sends me to a dark place of utter despair and rips me into pieces. And nothing reminds me more of Peter and my need for him than the weekend.

The weekend was always a time for Peter and me to reconnect, to connect, to be as one. My weekends fill up with idle time since Peter's death, and they bring about an emptiness so intense I shake from it. I feel the entire loss of him when I eat dinners alone, during my solo car rides, even while vegging in front of the television. I feel his absence during my sleep, and I am aware of it the first thing in the morning. My weekend consists of silent solitude and the high-pitched whines of vacancy that hurt my soul. It travels through me, torturing my being and forcing the devastation from missing Peter to gush out of me in a flood of tears.

Peter and I were both independent people, and our alone time was necessary and unique to both of us. But we always knew there would be time to spend with one another and reconnect on most weekends. Those were the times we would sit without words as we watched a movie or have all sorts of discussions eating dinner together. We felt each other's presence as we ran errands together in the car, and we were one during our intimate moments. These were the moments where we lived and breathed as a couple. They were steady times, warm times, times of attachment. But they are gone now, vanishing like the sun right before a sudden storm. I feel the ache of every gut-punching remembrance of what I have lost. I am alone now, and on the weekends, my loneliness is so very prevalent.

I have a lot of kind people in my life, people I love and who love me. Still, the number of people in my life compared to when Peter first died is starting to get smaller. Texts are fewer. Messages are less. My cell phone does not ring as often. And I get it. Their shock has worn off; their grief has lessened; their lives move on as it should be. I hold no anger, although, to be honest—and I'm always honest—I do hold disappointment for a few, the few I thought understood more. I try not to dwell on those few, though. I try to embrace the number of people who have realized even while my shock may have diminished, my life is still in flux as my grief is still here, especially on certain days, like weekends. I suppose those are the people who know me best.

I've been gifted in my life with kind people, and yet my hurt prevents me from reaching out to them. Many times, I don't even have a desire to be around anyone. As well-intentioned and loving as they are, they are not, nor will ever be, a replacement for my mister, my Peter, the source of my *once-was*. So, I ache and feel damaged because I am alone.

I never thought I'd say it, but I hate weekends. I once liked them when I had Peter in them. I know, eventually, I will be okay with them again. Maybe even feel a spark of excitement come some Thursday. But for now, my weekends are glimpses into the horrible nightmares of the holidays, birthdays, and anniversaries I face in the future. The times where isolation grabs hold of my heart and squeezes until I can't breathe. I'm glad tomorrow is Monday.

My Safe House

I'm leaving my house for a weekend getaway today. It'll be my first vacation since Peter died. My house has been my cocoon since Peter died. It's been my refuge from the outside world full of things that cause me despair and anxiety. It has given me courage when I needed it, and it's been my safe place to land when Peter's death pushed me into uncertain widowhood. My house is where the memories of him blanket me in comfort and sometimes cause pain. It's a house I know I will have to sell eventually because of its size and the upkeep I'm not willing to take on. I can't seem to commit to when I will sell, nor do I have to right now.

My house, which used to be our house, was the one Peter and I planted our family in for twenty-four years. It's where we grew our relationship, created, and built friendship, made love, had arguments, made up, laughed and loved and sometimes hated, and always accepted unconditionally. It was where I continued to commit to the vows I made in front of family, friends, and God, sometimes during the worst of moments. And after Peter died, my house was where I allowed myself to openly grieve without embarrassment. My house was my solace when Life became cruel, and I needed—I still need—a place to protect myself from all of the brutality.

I'm leaving my house today. I am trusting my son and neighbors to look after this place. Today, I am stepping out from the one place I feel safe. I am tearing myself away from security because it's time. It's time to unlock myself from this castle of grief, no matter how much I yearn to ball up and just exist.

I am a dreamer and a doer and a tough girl from the South Side of Chicago. I was Peter's dreamer and doer and tough girl from the South Side. I don't want to imprison myself in my house; Peter would have never wanted this for me. I know I can't stay stagnant. I know Peter would not want the woman he fell in love with and married to tether herself to this house and not be free in the world. It's not the woman he fell in love with. It's not the woman I love.

My bags are packed and in my car's trunk. In a few hours, I will head out of town. This is just the first of many weekends away in the next month. Not only do I have a birthday and an anniversary coming up that I don't want to be in the house for, but his weekend is my first of many attempts to dip my toe in the unprotected waters outside my safe house. My house served its purpose over the years, including now in my grieving times. It held my children while they grew, housed Peter and my relationship and all that meant, and soothed me when Death claimed the most important person in my life. While I don't want to fully let go of it, I need to start taking steps away from it if I am ever going to fully live again. I have to release it in order to live in the world of independence, where I should live. The way Peter would want me to live. The way I want to live. The way I have to live now in order to live at all.

PART II

See Me Grieve

I Am a Widow

I am a widow. I am a *widow*. I *am* a widow. No matter how I say it, *I am a widow.* This is odd to me. It's scary as hell and lonely and pissy. The definition comes with all sorts of baggage and horrible connotations—old maid, a woman to be pitied, scary lady in black, etc. But to me, admitting this to myself also means two other things. First, my life from now on will always be one without my husband, my steadfast, my co-parent, my lover, and my best friend. Always. This will never ever change. Second, my life has taken a turn from the road of what I thought was going to be—a fairly smooth road—to a road I don't know, near a cliff and headed God knows where.

By now, you might think I should get this, I am a widow. I mean, it has been a while. I should accept, or at least realize that I am a widow. I realize it, but I'm not so sure I can accept it.

Last night, I was out with friends at a local brewery for trivia night. It was almost fun. It helped that I'm fairly good at trivia. I didn't feel comfortable being out. Comfort is not my thing right now. I might have even come across as crabby. I am like that a lot lately—crabby. I try not to be, and yet, I am. I'm normally not a crab, but boy, did that change when Peter died. I was having a fairly decent time when out of the blue—seriously, out of nowhere—it hit me. I am a widow. I have no Peter. I have no husband. These realizations bitch-slapped me in the middle of a question about who the nurse took in the Farmer and the Dell. (The cow, by the way.) A few minutes later, during a break, I went to the bathroom and had a short cry.

I did tough it out and stay. I don't think my friends expected anything. I am getting good at crying on the inside. When I got home though, I released all of what was inside in loud, uncontrollable sobs. In the solace of my home, I feel free to let go of all I try to hide. It's my soft place to land.

At Target the other day, I was walking down the aisles, finding things to add to my cart that I don't need but, you know, it was Target. Target has this magical power of moving my hand onto things like dish towels and forcing them into my cart. As I walked, seeing nothing in particular to trigger me—no couple, no kid with her dad—and not hearing anything to egg me on—no love song, or missing you song—I started to cry. I cried from the words that popped up in my head: *I am a widow.* They came out of nowhere and sucker-punched my heart. And the tears came. Even after all this time, I don't need a trigger or an egging on.

While I was wiping down the kitchen counter the other day, tears bounced off the laminate top. One fleeting thought of *I am now without Peter, I am a widow*, and I was a goner. I let everything go. I let myself crumble into that all too familiar mess of emptiness and longing. Nothing says *"you are alone in this world of widowhood"* more than being a heaping pile of tears in front of your microwave.

Every night, before I go to bed, I am reminded I am a widow, I am without Peter. And it shocks me every single time. Maybe it's a picture of Peter hanging on my wall, the one I stare at and talk to as if he'll pop out. Or maybe it's the lonely steps up the stairs to my empty bed like some bad *Norma Desmond* reenactment, only the other way around. While I lie in my darkened bedroom, I can't wrap my head or my heart completely around the fact I will forever be without Peter and I will live as a widow.

I tell people I can't believe I'm living this life. I know denial is all part of the grieving process, only I'm not in denial. Not really. It's more like disbelief. I know Peter is dead. There's no denying it. The initial accident report, the death certificate, the lawyers, the insurance companies, the donations of his belongings, the absence felt every day, everything now reminds me Peter is dead. Oh, I know it. And I can't seem to comprehend that this is my life now. I can't seem to believe the unhappiness I am always living in. I can't seem to reconcile my life has taken a sharp turn away from what once was into the lonely unknown.

I have near-okay days, but then I'm tripped up by a memory, a realization, an out-of-nowhere feeling of life without Peter and being a widow. When it happens, I fall down hard in despair, in anguish, in aloneness. I suppose this is another part of grief's definition—the sudden change of mood or the constant change of mood.

Eventually, I will learn to live with my shattered heart. Despite having been my life since Peter died, this is all still so new. I continue to allow myself to feel and go through the pain. I logically know Peter died. What I don't get, what I will never get, is how this all happened in the first place, how I have no Peter, how I have no marriage . . . how *I am a widow*.

Stepping into Another Unknown

I went into his office, scared to offend him after all the kindness he showed me since Peter died. After I sat down and discussed some business, I said, "Bill, I'm going to quit this job." I finally told my boss what I've been wanting to say since this entire nightmare began. I am leaving my job.

It was not a decision based on the never-ending sadness widowhood brings. No, this decision was based on the never-ending desire of following my dream. This need has been in me since college and, happily, did not leave once grief overpowered so much of me.

See, I've wanted to write forever. And I still do, but it's not enough for me to be a five-in-the-morning writer or a weekend writer. No, I want to write all day. I want to make writing my full-time job. And make no mistake (as so many often do), writing is a job. It takes some talent, sure, but it also takes dedication, hard work, focus, meeting deadlines and resilience. Writing is with me 24/7. I write, plan characters, plots, settings, and think *What am I going to write next?* all the time. All. The. Time. Since Peter's death, my love of writing has not waned. I switched focus. I mourn the other focus.

Obviously, I am still writing, but not the comedic romances I normally write. I wrote those when I was happy and great with my full life. When Peter died, my life became the opposite, full of misery. My ability to write romances died when Peter died, for he was my muse. Writing like I once did has disappeared. I hope to find it again as I journey through this reluctant stage of life, but for now, that part of my writing is gone. Now, like always, I write what I know. Now, I know death. Now, I know widowhood. Now, I know a different, sucky life.

I'm not sure how my writing will look once I am dedicated to it full-time, and it scares me. Yet, Peter's death has taught me the future is not guaranteed. I can't keep pushing off what I want to do just because I'm scared. Really, what I live now, in my every day of widowhood, is scary. Luckily for me, fright is a great motivator. I can't say, "Oh, I'll wait a few years," because I may not have my next hour, let alone another tomorrow. If not now, when?

I've told a few people in my life when I was leaning toward this decision. Not everyone was like, "*You get 'em, girly.*" In fact, most felt the opposite. I understand and appreciate their concerns since it comes from a place of love. Writing is a solidary experience, one done alone, and some people fear I may become a recluse, which will add to my loneliness with Peter gone. But I am already lonely even when I am around people, and all I want to do is cry. Holding it all in sometimes is not the greatest for a heart-on-my-sleeve person like me. In response to their concern that I will waste my time putzing around, I say: writing is work, people, and even if I putz, putzing may be a way to think about writing; and/or putzing may be a part of my healing process. Finally, when they question my financial stability, I tell them I'll make it work. (Psst, plus my part-time job will not get me into the millionaire's club. Just saying . . .)

I know it seems like I am defending myself, to you, to my friends, and I don't owe anyone an explanation, but I want to explain, not defend. It may also seem like I am trying to convince myself, and maybe there's a bit of that, too. Still, the light bulb above my head keeps blinking, reminding me this is a step I have wanted to take most of my life. Now, as I have to redefine myself, find parts of myself hidden somewhere, and emerge with strength to face the unknown in front of me resulting from Peter's death, I want to take this step forward. I want to live in the now and not put life off into the future. I don't want my dream to go unfulfilled. I need this, now more than ever.

When I gave notice to my boss, he told me he was expecting it. Perhaps he sees how widowhood changed me; perhaps he knew I needed to leave in order to continue on this reluctant journey. It doesn't really matter what he thought, or others. What matters is, I am content with my decision. Sure, there's a little trepidation. I suppose that's always there when anyone takes a leap of faith, a leap into their dream. To the core of me, I am at peace with my decision. I don't know what I don't know until I know. I can't keep waiting or guessing on the unknown, waiting for tomorrow. I mean, I could, but I won't. Didn't Peter's death show me, tomorrows may never come?

Emergence

I slept in this morning. I think I'm a natural night owl anyway; my body adjusts when it had to—kids, jobs, whatever else. But when I don't have to, it's like my body dances in the freedom of the night. This is a change I'm learning to go with, letting my body do its thing. Last night, I stayed up until midnight and rose in the morning at nine o'clock. This schedule was different from the night before, and maybe it will be different tonight. Last night I made a different choice, one of many that will form the whole person I am supposed to be now, learning to live without Peter. A lot has changed in me since Peter died, and I am learning to go with it.

I have read and heard through other widowed women, once a spouse dies, what emerges will be different and new. Widows are never the same again. That may mean losing people in your life and gaining others. Or it might mean making choices, bad ones, good ones, and ones not everyone will understand or agree with. I already feel different. I already had to defend a major decision. Friends have already dropped out of my life, too uncomfortable to know what to do. I've already started my metamorphosis, and I'm only in the beginning stages. I don't know who I am or who I will become, but I will become someone different. Not a better someone, nor worse, but a different someone.

Of course, the major change is the missing half of me ripped away by Peter's death. Since he died, I've been walking around half-assed, half-everything. My humor that caused Peter to smile his crooked smile, to sometimes laugh even, is dimmed. My need to share everything in my life with him has been stripped away. I mean, I still "tell" him things, but I don't get a response, which makes me feel foolish. My relief in sharing life's load, and all that means, is finished. It's only me, and that sucks.

And then there are the finances. Those are no longer ours. Instead, they are mine, and it is completely and utterly overwhelming. It's like being in a foreign country, on my own, without speaking the language or knowing its culture, and unaware of my surroundings. I'm getting by in the finance department, even learning, but as a wise reindeer once said about his glowing nose, "It's not very comfortable."

There are the everyday changes that are neither good nor bad—just there. Like, I don't eat fruits and vegetables as much as I should. Okay, maybe that one is bad; they are good for me. I only eat now when I'm hungry and when I am, especially when I am hangry, vegetables and fruits are not what I want to fill me up. My diet now is cheese, ice cream, and hummus-related. Oh sure, I have gone to the grocery store once or twice and filled my cart with good foods like fish and chicken—I even ate lamb the other day—but mostly I grab what is fast and convenient . . . when I grab anything. You'd think I'd be stick thin by now, but no. My metabolism laughs at such a thought.

There are changes in my house. I actually keep a clean house. I'm preoccupied with a clean house sometimes. I guess since I only live in three rooms, it's not too hard to maintain. And let me say, by clean I mean by my standards: not pristine, just uncluttered and looking good. I've never been any type of '50s sitcom housewife. Not my thing. The second apartment I lived in on my own had a huge closet. It was almost like a third bedroom with no windows. I was dating Peter at the time, and whenever he came over, I would throw everything lying around the room into the closet. I mean *everything*. He opened it once, and I swear I heard the *Benny Hill* theme song as everything came pouring out of it. My point is, Peter knew of my housekeeping skills, or lack thereof, and still married me. He must have really loved me. How ironic that now he is gone, I keep a better house.

With Peter no longer part of my every day, I go out a lot more now with friends—for dinner, for tea, or for conversation. I'm sure it has to do with my need not to be in my house all the time. Peter liked his alone time, and I gave it to him knowing we'd come together eventually during the day or night. I tried to keep my nights open so we could be together. Now, there's no Peter for me to get together with, and God, does *that* hurt. There are times when it hurts so much, I back out of commitments to be alone in my misery. Most times, I really try. Sometimes the pain is too much, so I go home early. And there are also times, like last night's three-hour dinner, when it feels okay.

There are decisions I make now and will make in the future, without the consideration of Peter, only of me. I don't have to evaluate Peter's feelings or expectations in my decisions anymore. That just kicked me right in the gut . . . sigh . . . but it is the truth, as painful and sad as it is and as lonely as it makes me feel, it is the truth. Peter is not part of my decisions anymore. I recently designed my living room into something too modern for Peter's traditional taste but has always been mine. I quit my job to pursue writing full-time, a decision Peter wouldn't have supported for various reasons, but mainly because he was a realist. And really, writing doesn't make money. I think about renting in the city, an idea Peter abhorred and never would do when he was alive. I can even think about looking at Saugatuck, Michigan to rent, a place that didn't hold the same appeal to Peter as it did me. And my list goes on to the smallest things. My point is, it's all different now—how I live, my decisions, my future choices. All different.

I know some of these changes and decisions may not be the best for me—ahem, a lack of fruit and vegetables—and they may bite me in my widowed ass. I know some are based on emotion rather than logic, and I've always been the emotion to Peter's logic.

I know, I may fail. I also know, these changes and decisions may be the best for me now and not later, but the now is all I'm looking at. I am not a forward thinker anymore. My once-daydreaming self was killed when Peter was killed. And if I get bitten on my widowed ass, that's okay. As long as I can sit and stand and move, that's okay. If my emotions take over right now, at least I'm being true to myself. Emergence takes a long time and cannot be rushed.

New View

I did it. I rented an apartment in Chicago. And I am sitting in my writing chair, looking out at Navy Pier, in my new apartment. I have kept the house still but rented this place as sort of my vacation home. The move in day was just my daughter, the movers, and me. The movers were young kids, nice and polite. And the move went smoothly with a few hiccups here and there, but, as my daughter and I kept saying throughout this weekend, "We'll figure it out," and we did. It's been kind of our mantra since Peter died.

Everything is unpacked now. The cable and Wi-Fi are connected, pictures are on the wall, clothes are hung, and almost everything needing to be assembled is done. We kicked ass. We were like two Rosie the Riveters. The apartment is now ready for me to live in.

My daughter was an amazing support. I can't tell you how proud I am of her organizational skills and her patience for my lack thereof. She held me up emotionally as well. When we went out to dinner, she toasted me with words of encouragement, a nod to the past months, an acknowledgment of all that I did for her, her brother, and her father, and wished me the best in this new life of mine. All of what she said I needed to hear.

I'm still having some issues embracing all of this. I mean, before Peter died, I led a totally opposite, normal life with the man I loved. Now, I have different freedoms I don't know what to do with. I'm living in an apartment I feel as though I'm house-sitting for someone else. It's difficult for me to imagine a day of writing without interruption. It's all so surreal and massive for me to wrap my head around. Since Peter's death, I have said to friends and family, "I never wanted this, but here it is and so am I." In other words, I did not die with Peter. I am still living, sure in a life I didn't ask for, but it is what I have. I need to keep on keeping on.

The weekend was exhausting. Exhaustion should be added to the stages of grief. Of course, I was exhausted physically. This old gray mare who is out of shape took some hits with moving boxes, packing, going up and down stairs, etc. etc. And I was emotionally exhausted. Leaving behind the home I had, if only for some sort of an escape, and packing up some of my life without Peter into boxes, left its impact on me. As excited as I was to move to my apartment, away from the memories, and to heal in a different way, it also meant I was leaving a comfort. I was leaving my home, more or less.

I won't lie. I am worried here, alone in this city of my heart. I haven't been alone in over thirty years. As much as I have done on my own, almost everything was connected to Peter. Now, I am left alone in *my* life. This is my apartment. My bills I set up. It's all about my own choices from now on. My making it or breaking it without anyone to fall back on. Myself as my own security. There are a lot of *my*'s . . . too many *my*'s, and they're all scary as hell. It's not what I signed up or prepared for, and it goes against who I was for over the past thirty years.

As I sit and take in my life's new view, here's what I know. First, I will make it. I have to. After all this packing and unpacking, God, I have to make it, if only for a time. I don't have the stamina to do this again for a long time. Plus, I am a kick-ass woman.

Second, this new life has to be broken in before I can be totally comfortable wearing it. In the meantime, I have to enjoy the look.

Third, I need to push my apprehension of moving on. While the past is a mighty cozy friend and has enough power to yank me back sometimes, I know I have to continue, or else I will stand still in my grief.

Fourth, I don't know how to begin my new life. I still feel like a married, at-home, suburban mom. My definition has changed, and I have to embrace it. I suppose because it is the only way to be in it.

Finally, I feel guilty when contentment and happiness seep into me. I can't. This situation was handed to me. I never chose it. I never caused it. I never asked for it. I have to battle my feelings of guilt with these reminders as my weapon. I'm wielding them more and more, but not as much as I should. Guilt is strong in my life, and it's going to take many more battles to win the war against it.

When I moved into the apartment, I moved closer to living a life without Peter. My new digs won't take away my grief, nor will it miraculously cure me of my despair. I suspect new forms of angst, anger, longing, and sadness will still come. But I need to change my life's path in order for me to see the beauty in it again. And right now, sitting in my chair, writing, with the view of Navy Pier, I feel like I'm off to a great start.

Grief, You Fickle Bitch!

Well, it happened again. I cried in front of an unsuspecting soul. Before I get into the why and where, let me just say, grief is a fickle bitch. She is! No other word for her. She watches me ascend to the highs of doing something on my own, then slaps me down with another reminder Peter will never be with me again. I can't keep up with her. I roll with it, knowing she will level out eventually, but I don't like the ride.

So yesterday, I had a furnace person come out. I know it's a good thing to do a checkup on your furnace every year. Peter was the person to perform this (with his brilliant handyman mind), but since he's not around, I had to hire someone. Before the man even came out, I knew there would be some issues. I saw the rust, and the mold—thank you, leaky humidifier—and I heard the rattling when it whooshed on. The unit is getting into its golden years, so I was waiting for the bad news. He delivered it.

When he started to tell me all that was wrong including the rust, mold, and clattering, I cried. Right in front of him, I blubbered on about how Peter died suddenly, he took care of all of this and it's all too much. Poor guy. I wonder if he takes psychology classes with his furnace lessons. No matter. He listened and gave me advice on what to buy and what not to buy. (He actually pointed me to the less expensive one.)

After he left, I got into my car and drove to my apartment. Peacock feathers sprung around my car seat as I thought how driving downtown once scared me, and now it was as mundane as a drive in the country. As I drove, I thought, *You go girl. Look at you.* I even took a wrong turn downtown, but my muscle memory from working downtown for so many years led me to my apartment building.

I was about to settle in for the evening when I recalled seeing some flyers about a tree lighting event in the park by me last night. I thought it'd be nice to be part of a neighborhood thing and maybe get a little spark of Christmas cheer. I took a deep breath, got bundled up, and gave myself a pep talk.

What happened next seemed like it could be out of one of my novels. It is unbelievable, but I swear on any and all bibles, it happened. As I was approaching the place in the park where the event was happening, what should be blaring on the speakers but Elvis Presley's "Blue Christmas"! I laughed aloud, and hard. Of course, it would be playing. This was my life. I also saw Peter in my mind, with his eyes wide, a smile across his face calling out those fabulous lines around his eyes, and his laugh joined my own. The song was in its last verse, but there it was, blaring out the lyrics I knew to be true: "I'll have a blue, blue, blue Christmas."

When I found a place to stand near the playground, I watched parents with their kids in line to see Mickey and

Minnie and other kids playing in the snow, playing on the playground, and drinking hot chocolate. I was the only one without kids or a partner and I thought, *I wonder if people think I'm being creepy . . . especially after my belly laugh.*

I asked a lady standing near me, while her kids pushed each other down in the snow, what tree was going to be lit. She looked at me like I had asked where I could score some drugs and told me, "There is no tree. They light up the playground." *The playground?* Then I remembered, *I am in the city.* I stayed for the lighting of the swings and the slide, then left, still kind of chuckling.

In one day, in ten hours, I went from crying in front of an unexpecting furnace guy, to beaming with delight in finding my way without fear, to guffawing in front of a bunch of strangers while a park was being lit up. I am emotional. I don't know that I can do something until I have to. And I find humor in the absurdity of life. But, really, since Peter died, grief brought me to the sudden onset of these emotions, and within ten hours. She brings me to my knees in the deepest sadness I've ever known, then has me walking on the clouds from conquering an obstacle, to laughing at the ridiculousness of the turn my life has taken.

I know in my *eventually's*, I will even out, become stable. I will learn to live with the sadness, the victories will be part of my everydayness, and I will laugh at other things again. Until then, grief really is a fickle bitch . . . one I never, EVER, thought I'd have in my life like this.

Bye to Christmas

It's done. Christmas is over, and I am watching out for what lies ahead. I spent six days here in the home Peter and I built. In those six days, I scattered Peter's ashes, spent time with my children, went to see my mother, who thought my son was Peter throughout the visit, and I dragged myself through Christmas Eve and Christmas with a surprising sense of *"this-isn't-so-bad."* They were the longest six days of my life, and lately, my life has been stuck in one continuous loop.

This Christmas wasn't horrible, and it wasn't good. I didn't feel overly sad, overly grieved, nor did I hold excitement for the day. I didn't feel much of anything other than empty. I was devoid of any emotions. I didn't cry opening presents like I once did. I didn't get any joy from my kids opening their gifts like I once did. Nor did any type of excitement grow in my belly from our Christmas traditions. It was hard for me to feel anything with my emotional reserves emptied or turned off as I tried to push through the first Christmas without Peter.

The Christmas Eve dinner I always enjoyed was left untouched as anxious sadness robbed me of any appetite. Christmas Day, we tried something new. The kids and I went to see *Star Wars* and some of my tears fell. Going to see a science fiction movie was something we used to do as a family. We were missing part of the family. To be honest, I cried a lot about what I missed these past two days. Despite the crying, the days were better than I thought. Of course, it could be because I am so tapped out emotionally.

I was quiet a lot on Christmas Eve and Day. I am not usually like that. I never thought of myself as shy. But most of these past two days, I was out of words and emotions. I was a numb shell of myself. I don't know who the real me is anymore. I didn't think I would ever be this boring, mopey person with grief as my constant companion. Then again, I didn't think Peter would ever die this suddenly.

I didn't go to church this Christmas. I couldn't, as my faith is not important to me anymore. I'm not sure I'm even angry at God. I once heard anger described as disappointment. Maybe that's more accurate—I'm disappointed in God. I'm tired of pretending at every turn, including being comfortable in a church, to believe in a God I still struggle to understand and Her/His/Their ways. It is one of my grief hurdles to get over. There are so many ahead of me still. I know I want to get there, and maybe that counts for something. If I knew Peter was happy and with God, perhaps I would have jumped over that hurdle a long time ago. But I don't. I never will. So, I am still in training to jump.

The kids were terrific this Christmas. We all had grief hanging over us like some unwanted fog. But they were good, great in fact, excellent for sure. They filled my stocking like Peter used to do and gave me incredibly thoughtful gifts this year. My son gave me a tall drinking mug with my book's cover on it to match the one he got for me with my first book. He understands the importance of my writing. My daughter blew me away with a Kintsugi bowl. Kintsugi is a Japanese tradition. Broken pieces of pottery are assembled back together, and the cracks are filled with gold. My daughter explained how the bowl is reflective of my life right now. Peter's death shattered my life, and now I'm rebuilding it. I will have to live with the cracks and create something beautiful in the process, something golden. I know. I'm still in awe and touched by both of their beauty in gift-giving.

But it's all done now. The first Christmas without Peter is over. I went through another hard time. I feel the aftershocks of my emotions. The tears from grief and not-wanting-to-move are coming. I'm already looking at a veg day.

I know I have some busy days ahead of me. I am looking at a relaxing day today, maybe even napping. I think by January, I may collapse. Or maybe not. Time will tell. In the meantime, bye-bye Christmas. I made it through my grief of missing Peter.

Photograph

On the nights when I am in my house and not staying at my apartment, I touch a photograph of Peter before I go to bed. It hangs in the family living area of our house—damn it—my house. While my fingertips glide over his photo, I talk to him, or the picture of him, telling him about my day, asking him questions about where his spirit is roaming in the afterlife, trying to crack a joke or three depending on my mood, and then saying goodnight. It's been my ritual since Peter was killed. The photo is of us outside the Eiffel Tower in Paris on our twenty-fifth wedding anniversary. The picture gives me peace as it reminds me of our better times. And it gives me peace to talk to it, to touch it, to make it part of my bedtime routine.

Sometimes when I stare at the photograph, I look deep into his eyes. I like to escape in them, to see if I can find anything in them that lets me know he's alright. His eyes really were windows to his soul. They were kind eyes. This photo captures them well, and how I miss looking into those green windows. As Etta James sang, "Damn your eyes."

Peter hated being photographed. He never felt comfortable or authentic being photographed, and it shows in pictures of him. I've never been great about

SEE ME GRIEVE 101

being in photos either. It's probably why we decided not to have a photographer at our wedding reception. It was an odd choice to many, but all we wanted was to have fun. A person hanging around, snapping photos of us would have been torture. You can even see in the wedding pictures we did take our forced smiles and awkward poses. In some, we look like the couple from *American Gothic*. All that was needed was a pitchfork in Peter's hands and me in a gingham dress. But this photo of him in Paris captures Peter, in all his kind, gentle beauty, crooked smile and all. And I look like I'm beaming to be with him. It captured our spirit.

My one-way conversations with Peter's photograph are nods to our talks that would end our days. At dinner, or at the end of the night, we would summarize our days. Sometimes, we would rush through our summaries because our bedtimes were close. Other times, we would take long strolls through our days as we sat at the dinner table or went on an evening walk. Peter wasn't a huge talker, but sometimes, he would take his time recapping his day in one stretched out, beautiful prose. Other times, the synopsis of his day ended as quickly as it started. But every time, we shared our days, in short spurts, long completeness, or somewhere in between. And I miss that. I miss our shares, and God, do I miss his voice.

The hardest part of talking to Peter's picture is the absence of a response. Knowing him as deeply and long as I do, did, I can imagine his response. Still, it's not the same. It'll never be the same. And when I am in our house, on a particularly difficult and grief-riddled day, talking to his photo deepens my despair. Yet I do it anyway. It's become another new habit for now because of the comfort I find, even if it breaks me down to my core. Perhaps those are the times I need it even more.

Last night, alone in the house, like all my nights now, I talked to Peter's picture again. I asked how he liked the new chairs my daughter had reupholstered for me. I went on about my day, my plans for tomorrow, and finished by telling him the same thing I tell his photo every day: I ache from missing him. I kissed my fingertips and ran them over his thinned lips, his kind eyes, and his crooked smile. Then I went to bed.

Maybe this seems like an odd practice, to talk to the photograph of my dead husband. And maybe in the future I'll stop it. Or maybe not. I mean, it is harmless. And since Peter's unexpected and sudden death, I've learned not to look too far forward. So, for now, I talk to a photo of him, unabashedly and with purpose. Right now—all that I'm looking at—I can't just stop recapping my day with Peter. After all these years of sharing our lives at the end of the day, the withdrawal would be too painful. And I already have enough pain.

Friends Stayed and Went

I found out who my true friends and family are in all of this, the death of Peter and this widowhood I am now in. I suppose I have always known who would and would not be there for me, only now my lonely grief won't let me pretend or look away. The people who have stayed, even after their own shock and grief wore off, are my true, constant, and unconditional friends. The people who walked, ran away, or were never around when the most horrible thing happened to me and have not come near me since . . . well, they were probably never my friends.

I understand. People are uncomfortable with death. People have the right to move on and away from me. People are busy. People have crap in their own lives equal to, or even greater than, my own grief. I get all of it. Maybe I understand this all too well because I have done it to others. Three years ago, I did not show up for a friend when her brother died. I reasoned my guilt away with thoughts of my own struggles at the time. Still, my inability to push aside what I was going through to be present for her, has haunted me ever since. I know I should have been there. All the apologies in the world will never take away the selfishness of my absence. I am not proud, but I did it, and I have learned lessons for the future. We are all human. I have forgiven people and their flawed humanity, even understood it, but that doesn't mean I can just let go of my feelings of abandonment, my anger toward their betrayals. I am human, too.

I don't expect communication every day. A text here, a phone call there, even a social media message would help. Am I asking for too much? I don't know. Maybe I am. Too vain of me? Too selfish? Too needy? Maybe. Again, I don't know. What I do know is people have let me down since Peter died.

A fellow member in this unwanted club of widowhood told me I will lose and gain friends in the days, months, years after the death of Peter. There will be a thinning out of my circle of friends. I will allow new people into this circle and release others. I know, I know. I should concentrate on those who are still around and support me. The old me would, the old, positive me. Oh, I'm still old with grief aging me, but I'm no longer positive.

Since Peter died, I have become this clingy person I don't recognize. I am sure it stems from my loneliness brought on by the absence of him, and perhaps some jealousy of everyone else moving on while I am stuck in this misery I've been thrown into. I want people in my life, and I expect them to be here for me. I am angry at the people who never reached out, for whatever reason, or left me too early in my grief. I don't have it in me to try to figure out people's reasons in an attempt to forgive and release some my pent-up anger toward them. Not now. I'm not that strong, yet. I don't feel good about myself. I feel like I am watching another person unravel with neediness and anger, a person I don't know. But here's the thing: I am a different person without Peter, someone I *don't* know.

Going Through the Memories

The kids and I went through Peter's clothes. We emptied out our closet and his dresser drawers. It may seem early for some, to do this within a few months after his death. For others, it may seem late. Grief doesn't have a timeline though, and it was the right time for us, for me. It grew harder to look at Peter's clothes every day hanging in the closet in a cruel reminder of another time. I wanted to rip the Band-Aid off already, feel all the pain and move on, at least in this instance.

My kids kept clothing most meaningful to them. I kept others—one even still had his scent. I gave some to Peter's sister who asked. The rest of his clothes are sitting in my car stuffed in plastic bags, waiting for their new home at St. Vincent DePaul resale shop. I could have donated to a place near me, but I didn't want to see them locally. Not now anyway. Not while the scab has been ripped off.

With some of the T-shirts, PJs, robes and button-downs, the kids and I remembered stories of Peter. *This was the hoodie he wore when he was sick, or this robe when he was really sick. He wore this to that one jazz concert. Remember when we got this at the Chicago Bluesfest? I remember this T-shirt from when we pulled beer together at an event. Oh, and remember this one I got him for Christmas that he never wore?* We would

laugh with these stories, cry telling them, or became
quiet, almost out of respect in telling a story of when
Peter lived.

During our afternoon of taking Peter's clothes off of
hangers and out of drawers, we discovered other things.
We found old photos of friends from college, school
papers giving glimpses into his teen years, mementos kept
from vacations, notes and cards the kids wrote to him or
scribbled their names on, and—the hardest discovery—
the old love letters I wrote to him.

Peter kept all my letters. I found them on the bottom
of a box in the back of the closet. They weren't tied neatly
in a bow in sentimentality; that was not Peter. They were
clumped together in a random pile. I read them to my
kids, editing out the juicy stuff. I needed to read the letters
to them, as if they needed to hear about our past, our life
before kids. Some of the letters were written during the
six months Peter lived in Portland when we only saw each
other every other weekend. We were dating exclusively
and had already confessed our love for each other. We did
long-distance and we made it work . . . before cell phones
and Facetime/Skype/Zoom.

The words I wrote, especially during the Portland time,
rung of familiarity. I wrote about my deep love for him,
how I would love him forever, and how much I wanted to be
with him again. The letters contained endless paragraphs
describing my desperate longing, my love, physical ache
for him, and my need to see him again. My newly-in-love
self at twenty-eight captured my widowed self of today.
I hold the same ache, desperation, longing, and love for

him today, only deeper. I want Peter back, so much, to see him and hold him. And even though Peter is dead, I know my love for him will always remain. The letters weren't my best writing, but boy, they were prophetic.

The letters comforted my heart with the realization that Peter had kept all my letters and cards. Through the years, he eventually threw out birthday, Valentine, anniversary, and Christmas cards. (Once he suggested for Valentine's Day we go to a drug store to pick out a card for each other, read it and put it back. He was kidding . . . I think.) I understood keeping a card only for a time because there would be so many over the years, and we said all we had to say in our years together. To be honest, Valentine's Day and Christmas were no longer celebrated with a card. But he did keep the letters and cards from the beginning of our lifelong love affair and to know this, to reread them, felt like Peter was with me yesterday, assuring me of his love from the beginning.

I texted my girlfriends about the letters. I told them I kept all of Peter's letters too, which meant I kept two. Peter wasn't much into writing them, and that was okay. It wasn't his love language. Although he never said anything about the letters, I feel he appreciated them by the mere fact he kept them for all these years.

Yesterday was a necessary day. It was not an easy day. Hurt, sadness, nostalgia, and deep grief were unwelcome guests yesterday afternoon spent with my children, Peter and my children. Afterwards, wanting alone time, I lay on the bed, hugging a hoodie still carrying his scent, and cried and talked to Peter and cried some more. But it wasn't all bad. Really. As my daughter said, it was hard to go through his things, yet there were happy moments in remembering. Those were the moments where Peter was alive for us, if only in a memory.

Half Year Now

It has been six months since Peter died. Looking back on this half of a year, here is what I know.

I miss Peter today as I did when he died. I have learned to live my pain, but I will never stop hurting or ignoring the loss of him in my life. Every day I carry the shock of his sudden departure from life. I have built myself up enough, more than when this all first began, to at least be adequately standing to accomplish things and move on.

Being a widow is an act I must perform alone on my life's stage. I have the support, kindness, and friendships of so many people. There are people in my life who have watched me, held me up, and caught me when I fell. They are in my audience, waiting to help. I still am in awe of all I have received from the people in my life. There are times now where I need to rely on them less because I must learn on my own how to live without Peter in my life.

My apartment downtown is my place to escape and regroup. I adore the views, feel its comfort and healing. I am lucky to be staying here when I need to recover and try to figure out how to live again. I would give this apartment back with its view and comfort, to have Peter back. But he's not coming back, and the apartment is doing what is best for me.

I am still living in a fog of uncertainty. I have no immediate or future goals right now, nor any energy to set any. These past six months have exhausted me. I am a dreamer, and I don't have the zest to even dream anymore without Peter in them. Until I gain strength, I don't care. I have to get through the day. In the evening, when I go to bed, if *"this day wasn't so bad,"* I will feel accomplished in my fog.

Finally, I am learning more about myself than I ever thought possible. During this most difficult part of my life, I am growing to understand more. The strong dependency I had on Peter once so strong is now gone. I allowed myself to be swept up in Peter's protection. It was Peter's love language, and I enjoyed hearing it. I never thought I would be without him or outlive him. But that happened.

Six months ago, God, the Universe, Death, dumped on me this life I didn't want or ask for, but here it is. And look at me. I'm still here. I cannot tell you how much this amazes me. Besides the birth of my two children, this has been my biggest accomplishment in life. And one I hold onto when I feel myself slipping into the *"I just can't anymore"* moments. I can, and I have for this half-year without Peter.

What Road Is This?

Now what? That's the question I keep asking myself. Since Peter's death, I have spent my life in shock, paralyzed with sadness, anger, disbelief, and longing. And lately, as I am learning to settle into my grief, I wonder what I do next, in my life without Peter.

My grief hasn't gone. It hasn't even slowed. It has become a part of me the way gravity pulls down my body to Earth. I don't like it, but disliking it doesn't make it go away, so I have to figure out how to move with it. I have to determine how to go through life without Peter. He's not coming back. He's not going to pull a *Lazarus*. He's gone from me, and as much as it sucks, hurts, and brings deep sadness to me every day, every single day, I need to learn to move, to just move. I need to manage to breathe in the toxic world life has handed me, because it's the only air I have to survive in.

Living now will be painful. It is already painful, and I don't think it'll ever go away. Like ever. I loved that man to the core of me. The pain may lessen, but the absence of him will always remain. However, like the athlete I once was, I have to push past the pain and play in the game of life. It's the only way I can survive, and for now, survival is all I have. There may be better than okay moments, even some giddy ones, even some joyous ones. And soon,

I hope, my emotions' muscle memory will switch from my survival instinct to living. It's something other widows talk about, the eventuality of living again. That'd be nice. Of course, they also say there's a long road to travel to get there. I am thinking I'm going to get carsick along the way, probably even bored and impatient. So, my question is: what do I do while I am on this road?

I don't know if preoccupations will help. I don't know if avoiding emotions will do any good. But that won't happen anyway because my heart found a home on my sleeve the moment I was born. I don't think distractions will aid much on this road of mine. I don't know if numbing myself with cleaning or watching TV or shopping or wine or writing or reading or fill-in-the-blank will be of any assistance. I don't know what I will do or how anything will help since I've never been on this road before. I don't know.

I never wanted to take this route, but here I am, so I better buckle up. There's no turning back. There's no Peter to take this wheel. There's no we, as a couple, to decide together or support each other. It's just me to face what lies ahead. Sure, I have my friends and kids to help me along the way. But they can't drive me for me, and they can't even be in the car. That's all me. It's a solitary trip since grief is unique to everyone.

My second romance book, *Wanna Bet*, has been out for a few months. I am putting some thought into selling my house and am ready to buy a new, smaller place. I am renting an apartment in the city, far from the memories housed in what was our home. I have some decisions to make about decluttering things accumulated throughout a marriage, a marriage I no longer have. I have to make important financial decisions and understand I will now have the social life of a suddenly single person. I have to see my life as it is, not as it once was, and all that means. This will all be hard for me. I'm not used to being single-minded. I am not accustomed to basing choices and decisions on me. They've always been constructed in the "us" of Peter and me.

I know I have to get some of this done in my future moments. The marketing for my book is a must-do if I want to be successful. After the long and laborious task of creating the book, I want to be successful. I also know I don't have to do all of my other tasks now, maybe not even a year from now. Only, I feel a need to tackle them tomorrow or in many tomorrows. It will give me a sense of control. My life veered out of control, so for me to grab it and steady it, if only in mental notes, is healing. Maybe there's even a sense of anticipation, which I try to square with my guilt in moving on. Which is ironic because Peter was the constantly moving man I married. He wouldn't want me to sit still. Honestly, I don't know if I could if I wanted to, as it not something I am capable of doing.

The bottom line is, I am beginning to look at *what-now's*. I am not done grieving. I don't think I'll ever really be done. I am ready to have grief as my constant companion, one that moves with me instead of keeping me in the same paralysis of pain. As painful and anxious and sad as those movements are going to be, I think I am ready to try. I'll have days and weekends where it'll all be too much, and I'll stop moving again. Those are the times I have to conjure up memories of Peter, and all he has set up for me, however painful, and continue to drive solo on the road of unknowns.

Getting Used To It

There is a certain getting-used-to this life as a widow. I think I'm starting to grow accustomed to my life without Peter. I don't like it at all. I wish with every part of me it wasn't like this. I am still sad. I am still lonely. Yet in all of this, all this widowhood and living life with a broken soul, there is a certain small acceptance, a certainty that this is my life now.

I think this began a few days ago. It was a silly little thing actually. I went grocery shopping and bought two bananas instead of a bunch. I didn't break down and cry about it. Later I cried, but not in that moment. I'm not sure if it was about the bananas. Sometimes I cry without even knowing why. Maybe it's grown to be a habit, this crying of mine. Or it could have been a delayed reaction. Whatever the reason for the crying, putting two bananas in my grocery cart seemed rote. I didn't give it a second thought.

I went to a wine festival with two friends yesterday. It was a festival Peter and I had gone to a few years back. I have clear memories of the day with Peter—the weather, the bumping into a coworker, the tasting of the wines, and the purchases of a few bottles of wine. I remembered it all. Yesterday, when I went, those memories were jogged, yet I somehow held it together. I'm not sure if I even felt like crying. I talked about it with my friends as if I were repeating a favorite childhood memory. I felt sadness, which I think I'll always feel talking about Peter, but I didn't break down, and I continued to have an okay time.

This morning when I awoke, I greeted the day knowing Peter would not be waiting downstairs for me. He would not be reading the paper as I went into the kitchen to make my tea. He would not be saying good morning. He would not be looking over his reading glasses as I carried my tea to my writing chair. (Yes, I have one.) It didn't shock me. It gave my belly a flip in loneliness and made me unhappy to have another morning without Peter. It probably always will. Yet I made my tea knowing this is how it is now—no Peter. No look of him, no smell of him, no taste of him, no feel of him. None of him. I am getting used to this no-Peter life. It sucks. It hurts. It devastates. It does all sorts of not so good things to me. And yet, I know this is my life.

Acceptance is another stage of grief. I get that. No one ever said those stages don't hurt, nor that they are consistent, that each one hurts less than the last. Stages of grief weave themselves around my tapestry of life at unexpected times and without uniformity. Acceptance is no exception.

I fear acceptance the most because it closes the door to all possibilities, leaving me more vulnerable. Accepting I have to live a no-Peter life means there's a finality in it all. When I had anger, I didn't really have to think about moving on, moving on without him. Denial meant I hung onto Peter. I skipped the bargaining stage so far, but it might come. I have a hard time knowing what I would bargain for, or who I would bargain with. And depression is a constant in my life since Peter died, something I am trying to get past in counselling. But this acceptance thing, this getting used to it? I think that's the scariest of them all.

Just because tears don't come with acceptance doesn't mean I feel any less pain than with the other stages. Only when you get beat up enough in life, you stop caring about the punches. Life has been relentless in pounding me with the absence of Peter. I've learned tears don't bring Peter or my life before back. So, I am getting used to feeling this way, knowing Peter won't return. I am creating a callous wall for protection. Walls always block out the unwanted. I suppose that's my survival mode right now. There is no other choice but to survive.

This is how I've felt lately, how I feel today. As I've learned, my feelings can change tomorrow, at the next sudden turn. I know as I continue to grieve, I will blow up with tears and anger and despair again. I will puddle into a heaping ball of messed up. Grief doesn't let go of you that easily, that fast. At least I know for me that's the case. My history has shown I go through a smooth patch of being okay, only to crash into large barrels of horrible. That's been my ride. But lately, despite still feeling the pangs of grief, there is an increased acceptance that this is my life now.

Yeah, I am getting used to living this not-so-great life of widowhood. I'm exhausted. I'm all over the place. And I'm missing Peter, terribly. But I am living. I'm living a life and getting used to this no-Peter life. I have a waterfall of emotions, changing currents all the time . . . and I'm starting to get used to those as well.

No Doubt, I Am My Mother's Daughter

Yesterday, I went to see my mom in the assisted living facility she calls home. When I got to her room, my mom was asleep in her wheelchair with the Catholic Mass blaring on her television set like white noise. I stared down at her, a woman I barely know anymore because senility and dementia have robbed her of what I knew. As I looked, I took in all the beautiful memories of our past, all the wisdom I received from her and all the reasons she remained my hero. I shook her shoulder gently, saying, "Ma, it's me, Betsy." Her eyes sprung open, with confusion, maybe even suspicion. Once recognition unrolled across her face, she smiled and cooed, "Oh, Betsy. So good to see you."

I dragged a chair over to where she sat, muted the TV per her request, and we talked. We talked about my apartment, about my kids, about how she was feeling, about the weather, and about my siblings. We also talked about her meals, and she repeated a few times she liked where she now lived, as if it was a new place, when in actuality, she had lived here for over three years now. We talked and talked and talked some more. She seemed better this visit than the last. There was more lucidity in her speech. She repeated herself often, and she forgot some names, but she was doing good, her own version of good.

There was a lull in the conversation, a pause which
served as an opening I needed to take advantage of.
I wanted to finally tell her something, something I've
wanted to say since Peter's death. Before she slipped back
into the nonsensical, I began to tell her about the journey
I started on when Peter died. I described my numbness,
my sadness, my denial, and how this was the worst I've
ever felt before in my life. I explained to her, in the weeks
that followed Peter's death, I didn't know how or if I was
going to make it. Even now, I didn't know what my life
would look like.

And then I told my mother something I needed to tell
her. I told her that she was what got me going again. Her
strength as a woman who held her family of nine together,
took care of her children, nursed my father while he slowly
deteriorated in health, and even took in her mother and
aunt when their health failed. She did all of these things
with love, patience, and resolve. I called her a woman of
grace when her husband eventually died. I explained that
her ability to move on without her husband and build her
own life after gave me courage. I told my mom she was
my rock and had been an example to me all my life. I
witnessed over and over again her incredible capacity to
carry on regardless of the burdens life weighed her down
with. All of her and all of what she had done were what
got me moving again. I said to her that when I started to
rise, I did so with the thought, *I am my mother's daughter.*
I got this. I said, "Mom, I have your amazing strength
and blood running through me, and that will gave me the
ability to power through all of this."

When I was done, my mom's eyes clouded up and her voice shook. She took my hand in hers and she said, "I really needed to hear this. Thank you." Then she raised my hand to her lips and kissed it. In those moments, she heard me, and I felt heard by her. But they passed as quickly as they came when her question of, "And how is Peter?" let me know she had slid back behind the curtain of confusion. I followed her along without correction, responding, "I think he's fine," and then sat to listen to her stories that were real to only her.

When it was time for my mom to go to the dining room for lunch, the nurse's aide came to take her. The aide smiled at me and said something they all say every time I visit: "You look just like your momma. No doubt you are her daughter." And there is no doubt . . . I am my mother's daughter.

Until Death Did Part Him

It still blows me away when I remember Peter is gone, he is dead, and for the rest of my life, I will be without him. I don't always allow it to sink in. The finality of all of this enters into my mind and heart like a flash that I can't let lie there. Denial? Not sure. Self-preservation? More likely.

Peter's Facebook account is still up. I'm not sure how to delete it. I'm not sure I want to. There's something connective about his page still lying there in the cloud as if he is still out there. I still post to it. Maybe it's my version of laying flowers at a headstone. Yesterday, I posted a quote stating he did love me until death did us part and will continue to love me. It was a beautiful quote, one I actually had been thinking about for a while now. To think he loved me until death did take him is a spectacular thought.

A few years back, a friend of mine was devastated when his girlfriend broke up with him. After comforting him, I told him what a hard but beautiful thing it was to feel so deeply. It meant he loved. It meant he was loved. My grief for Peter wouldn't be so hard if we didn't love so hard. I am beginning to realize the gift that was given to me, a gift not everyone is lucky or blessed enough to receive.

When Peter first died, in the midst of my pity and anger and grief, I questioned if he loved me. Not liked me, not loved me like a friend or a sibling. But whether he loved me deeply, like a partner, a lover, a wife. Peter wasn't very demonstrative, especially in public, and he wasn't full of pretty words or trinkets. It wasn't him. I once asked him during a romantic scene in a movie, "Why don't you say things like that to me?" He responded, "Because I don't have a writer to write them for me." Yeah, I laughed too.

With the suddenness of Peter's death, there was no final "I love you." Those words lie unspoken in a pile with goodbyes and other silent affirmations. I wanted the final "I love you," the "we had a good marriage," the "thank you." But it didn't happen like it does in the movies because there are no writers to our story. Instead, I am starting to see Peter's love language upon reflection and what remains. The flowers he planted because they were my favorite still bloom. My favorite meal of seafood and rice he made because he knew. The wooden bench he made for me, the one I bumped into every morning. The trust I know he had in me whenever I went out without him. The financial decisions he made that have kept me secure even after his death. His tentativeness during our intimate moments. And while I knew he spoke a different love language when he was alive, I am finally learning to decipher it, after his death.

As I am learning to live with this broken heart of mine, I am starting to realize the gift I had been given. The gift of loving him, of receiving love from him, of having each other's love when things went wrong or became difficult.

I experienced deep love, the kind of love two people share as partners in life. I was gifted something rare and beautiful. An unconditional, trusting love we carried for each other until death did part us. He had loved me from the first day he told me he loved me until the end of his life. How lucky am I?

Among the Stuff

I had a meltdown yesterday right in the middle of my basement. I was removing clothes from the dryer to fold, and I lost it. There is so much stuff in my basement that I am overwhelmed by it all. There are boxes of memories labeled "Peter" I need to go through. There are tools stacked up along the side of the laundry room, and I have no knowledge of their purpose. There is a box in a corner, never opened, addressed to Peter. When I opened it, I saw a part for some sort of thingamajig with a packing slip from 2013. There are boxes chock-full of mysterious objects so foreign to me, I'm thinking Peter led a secret life as a space explorer. I wonder if the Mars Rover might be missing some of its devices. There is an amazing amount of Peter and his stuff packed into this house, and the enormity of it all led to my meltdown.

I don't have sentimental attachment to any of Peter's junk, I mean, stuff. I don't even know the use for half of his stuff, maybe even three-fourths of it. I don't see an object and say, "Aw, that was used in the 1996 flood." It's more like, "What UFO biopsy was that used for, and does the government want it back?" Even if the tool was used for something I remember, I still have no emotional loyalty to it. You served your purpose, thank you and then, bye-bye. I don't think, *well, maybe in seven years I will need this*—unlike Peter. It's not how my mind works.

I'm not saying all his stuff is like that. I understand keeping the table saw from his father, even other tools handed down from his dad. Peter loved and respected his father. His father taught him a lot. His father's tools will definitely end up with my son and my daughter. They are part of their history, their connection to their father and his ancestry, their ancestry. I'm not a total tool snob. I just don't know what I would do with the replacement hose to a sump pump removed five years ago.

As I looked around the basement yesterday, overcome with the singular question of *where do I begin?* I could hear Peter's voice saying, "It'll come in handy one day." To his credit, once in a while, he did find uses for an object from 1993 or the whatchamacallit from 2004. Peter truly was a genius when it came to fixing things and recycling the old to repair the new. He was an amazingly gifted handyman. I always said, I break it, he fixes it. Another part of our interdependent flow. (He wasn't always happy about that flow. It put a lot of pressure on him to be the fixer all the time. He often thought if I paid more attention, or was not so impatient, things wouldn't break. Sigh.) However, most of the stuff he kept just piled up like a corner of a junkyard, and now, I look at it and think, *where the hell do I begin?*

It's overwhelming enough to deal with sudden widowhood. Besides the unspoken last goodbye and the final I love you, when a death happens instantaneously, like Peter's, an inventory on what he leaves never happens. He was alive one day, knowing eventually, things would be sorted out. He died the next, collapsing everything in my world, including small and large confusing objects. I was not told to save this, get rid of that, these are important, those can go. I wasn't told the sentimental attachment he had to some of the stuff. I don't know the value or importance of so much of what he kept. I don't know for certain the real reason why he held onto this or that, if there even was a reason. Those stories and explanations were being saved for the eventually which never came. And now, like yesterday, I stand in a basement filled with his stuff, without him to help me sort.

I know this isn't a race. There's no finish line for me to cross in the victory of getting my house or my life in order. I get that. I also know there will come a time when I need all this stuff to leave the house. My kids may want to keep a chunk of Peter's things, maybe put them in some storage unit for future use, like their father. They're both brilliant like that too. Hell, I may want to keep some of it. Maybe I'll face an alien one day. But I will still have to sort and go through it, deciding what will go and how to let it go. When I do, I will be releasing more of Peter, his inner *Fred Sandford*, which I teased him about, adored and admired in him and loved him for.

My kids may or may not help me sort through these things. I hope they do, but I hesitate to ask. I want my kids to grieve and heal first and foremost. Yes, I am protecting them and coddling them. Their father was killed. I probably could ask friends to help. Asking . . . what a concept. I know these options would help ease my feelings of being overburdened, yet they won't take away the overwhelming feeling of letting go.

The inevitable sorting, the letting go, the amount of it all—it all overwhelmed me yesterday and I broke down. In the middle of the basement, fits of tears and screams, asking how Peter could have left this all for me, I broke down. Realizing I will never have any answers from him, that I was alone in this, made my sobs come out harder. It was one of those moments of widowhood, of grief, that bitch-slaps you to the ground. And yesterday, I couldn't help but fall among all his stuff.

Sometimes I Wish

Sometimes I wish I could stop talking as if Peter were still living. I used to quote Peter and tell stories about Peter. He peppered most every conversation I had with others. His brilliant thoughts coming out of his brilliant mind crept into my conversation some way, somehow. I still slip him into conversations as if he were still living. I understand he'll always live in my thoughts and heart, but I mean, really living, in person with me. And when I do talk about him as if he were still living, it hurts more when I am reminded he's not.

Sometimes I wish people understood the true impact of Peter's death. I wish they were more gracious, more understanding, more aware of his absence in my life and how I am still mourning him. Sometimes I have higher hopes in people than they actually can deliver.

But then I also wish people didn't tiptoe around me. I wish an invitation would be offered to me without fear of how it would make me feel. I wish they would realize how important it is to be asked over, to do something, even with their caveat of, "I know it'll be hard, and I understand if you can't." I wish people had a balance.

Sometimes I wish I could let go of the disappointment I have in the people who should have been there for me during this time. Yes, I am so blessed by so many, especially my sisters by choice. They filled the gaps left by others and then some. They did so wonderfully, and I would have never made it this far without them.

Sometimes I wish I knew ahead of time how my mom is going to be when I visit her. I wish I could know if I will have the mom who can keep a conversation going, delighted to see me, engaging, and remembering Peter died. I wish I knew if I would have a visit like today, one where I spent time convincing her she wasn't dead and then more time comforting her when she said she wanted to die. Perhaps if I did, I would avoid the latter visit because it rips apart my already fragile heart to think how unfair Death was to take someone who wanted to live and leave behind someone so ready. Sometimes I would like to know so I can selfishly decide.

Sometimes I wish I had the right words of comfort for my children, and I wish I knew how to deliver them. I know their grief is deep, and I would be much happier if I could heal them like when they skinned their knees. But it's their hearts that have been shredded, and I don't know the words, or the way, or the place to plant kisses to make it all better. So, I carry their pain on top of mine and sometimes, that hurts more.

Sometimes I want to convey my needs without hurting others. I want to express what I need to get done in order to move on, in a way that doesn't overwhelm or put anyone in the position of guilt or anger. It seems I fail many times, and sometimes I wish I knew how to map it all out before my delivery.

Sometimes I wish I didn't have my good days. I wish

them away because the bad days always loom and it's then I realize, I'm not done grieving. I wish I could have all the bad ones at once, get them over with, so the good days could stay with me and I would never have to slip back into the bad. Sometimes the good days just serve as a tease, and I'm too tired to be played with.

All the time, I wish for my life with Peter back. A life I could count on—a life with the cuddles and the fights and the mundane. All the time, I wish for Peter and his brilliance, his comfort, his humor, his feel, his taste, his everything back with me . . . all the time.

Seeing Him Whole

Last night, I missed Peter. I missed him bad. It came over me like a sudden gust of wind, chilling my soul. It's not that I stopped thinking about him and his absence. But yesterday I missed Peter because, lately, I've been thinking more about our marriage—all of it, including the ugly moles on it.

In the beginning, when Peter first died, I saw only his beauty and the dazzle in what we had, since that was what I was missing. Lately, though, I've been thinking about Peter's flip side. We all have one, right? I mean, I do. My impatience is loud and nasty. Sometimes, it causes me to snap, like an angry alligator. I can be rude. Oh, I can be, let me tell you. I have unreasonable expectations, am super sensitive, and also I can . . . let me get back on point. Peter had his flaws too, and maybe as part of my process of moving on, I need to face those as well.

As I start my new life, I have to realize *all* of what was left behind. I think taking an honest look at the whole is a part of grief no one really talks about. People adhere to this *"don't speak ill of the dead"* philosophy, maybe not to offend or hurt the survivors. Perhaps, a memory tarnished is too hard to admire. I don't know, but no one speaks openly about the flaws of the person who has died. Only, I feel honest observations and reflections will show a whole person.

It's hard to look at the entire being, especially someone you will never see again. It has been for me. It's hard for me to admit Peter wasn't perfect. I held him in such high esteem, almost idolized him. When he died, that grew for me as if he gained legendary status. But then, lately, there came these wait-a-minute moments. For instance, with my second book published now, I thought about the times where Peter wasn't supportive of my writing. I am not sure he ever fully embraced the writer in me, and writing is a huge part of who I am. His lack of enthusiasm for my writing left me, at times, feeling rejected.

There were other instances as well, other things he said to me or ways he treated me that I didn't appreciate. And I know I was not the perfect wife either at times. Every marriage has moments when it takes effort to mend in order to stay in the marriage. Lately, I have been remembering those moments. They had come before, every now and then, and I had batted them away like annoying gnats getting in the way of my worship for him. In this past week, however, I couldn't even shoo them away. I let them come. I needed to let them come.

I needed them to come to understand the things I will not be missing about Peter. Of course, I would take his flaws back in a heartbeat if it meant having Peter back. Still, there are arguments, annoyances, misunderstandings, frustrations, and difficulties I will not miss. This recognition is important to me in order to move toward healing and acceptance.

My willingness to reflect on our entire marriage arrived during a time when I'm trying to figure out my comfort without him. Grief often throws different things at me depending on where I am in the moment. Right now, grief is throwing this honest look my way because I'm ready to take a peek. It hurts, sure, and I have regrets. In this introspective on the not so good parts, I also have to take a look at the role I played because marriage is not an independent institution. I know this. But in regards to Peter's flaws and shortcomings, seeing them doesn't make me think any less of him. It actually makes me miss him more.

I know that sounds weird, to miss the flaws of a person. I thought so . . . until I reread what I wrote in my third book last night. I wrote this before Peter died. I let the book lie for a while, and recently, I started to chip away at it again. I read this one passage where the main character, in her inner dialogue to the reader, says, "Flaws are part of the whole of a person and you have to love these parts to love the whole." And she's right. Flaws are part of the whole. Peter's flaws were parts of his whole, and I loved him wholly. Damn, my characters are smart. (Of course, she does not mean abuse. That's not a flaw; that's evil and illegal.)

Peter's flaws just make the memory of him all the more real. He was real. What we had was real. If I only saw his beauty, if he only saw mine, we would have the phoniest marriage on the earth, with the exception of some reality stars. But we didn't. And seeing his flaws now, in the light of widowhood, grief is giving me all it has to offer.

I don't think it's a coincidence this acceptance of the whole comes at a time when I am starting to figure out where I am to go from here. This may be another healing point. It could be I'm at a turn in the road of grief and I'm headed to a smooth part . . . before I'm thrown into another turn again. Maybe I have time now that things have settled a bit to reflect on everything. I think more and more about Peter, the person, and the husband. Or possibly, it's a stage in grief left out, a secret one no one wants to admit to, as if a person's flaws or an imperfect marriage should be shameful.

This double-take at the wholeness of Peter and our marriage is what I needed. I needed to see Peter wholly in order to grieve him entirely.

If

Sometimes I play this morbid game. I ask myself: what if Peter did not die? What if he was still alive? How would that look? I block out the voices that say, *this is stupid because he is dead*, and *don't make it harder on yourself*, and I put myself in the moment of the question, in the now. Maybe this isn't the mindfulness therapists teach, but it's my own, macabre game. And here's what I think it would look like.

If Peter were still alive, I would be working at a job I didn't hate. I would be bored, frustrated I didn't have more time to write, looking forward to Thursdays at noon when I could relax with a three-day weekend, but I wouldn't hate it. I would be content. And I would be repeating to myself and others how lucky I was to have the job which didn't require too much out of me, with a wonderful boss, and that Peter and I had the means for me to work part-time. I know I would because this is what I did, every day, when Peter was alive and working, hard, for us. And if he were still alive, I would continue my gratitude, every day.

If Peter were alive, I would not feel the depth of my appreciation and love for special people in my life. I would not fully understand their kindness, unselfishness, and unconditional love for me. I would not be in awe of their generosity when they came running to pick me up and stayed to hold me up and keep trying to formulate the right words of thankfulness. Yet, if Peter were alive, I also would not be feeling deep hurt and anger at the people in my life who were absent when I needed them the most. I would not know the devastating disappointment by those I thought I knew, but now realize I never had a clue.

If Peter were alive, my kids would not be suffering. They would not have their bouts of paralyzing grief or despairing longing for their father. They would talk to their father every week at some point, and he would dole out his opinion or wisdom in his understated, calm way. He would help them grow as a man and a woman in their twenties. And when we all got together, we would be the tight-knit family of four so many people strive to have in life, and few are lucky enough to achieve. If he were still alive, my kids' pain would not be so raw.

If Peter were alive, I would be back in my life of security and fulfillment. I would eagerly anticipate intimate moments and the opportunity to bask in every drop of his love for me. I would laugh more and cry way less. I would talk more and not be silenced by the aloneness of my day. I would experience the good and the bad in life with him. I would be balanced by his half and would not be dizzied by the disparity of my world.

If Peter were alive, I would not know my deepest grief. I would only know the grief of those who have died in my life—a father, a grandmother, an aunt, a friend—but not the grief which stopped my life because Peter was my life. He was in every part of it. If Peter were alive, I would continue living as the person who I knew as me and not have to stop to face, to discover a person I don't know anymore.

If Peter were still alive, I would continue to be happy. I wouldn't know the pain his absence caused, and I could go on. Sure, I may take him, us, for granted, but I would also recognize he was my perfect match. And even with the bouts of nagging, arguments, and the times of turning away from each other, the warmth of knowing he stayed with me as my touchstone, would drift over me at unexpected times. And in those moments, I would feel my purest form of happiness.

There is gratitude I get from What If, the playing out of these scenarios in my head. It comes from understanding all that I received from Peter. It comes from the blessing of my being chosen as his till-death-do-us-part person. And it comes from the light Peter left burning inside of me, one I will keep with me, and use it to warm people along the way.

There is a peace from the game, too. Perhaps it helps me deal with the grief of knowing it's all contrary to what I'm living. Perhaps it gets me closer to a life which Peter is no longer a part of. Perhaps peace comes from knowing what I had. Or perhaps it settles me, grounds me, pushes me to continue on. Looking back is one way to move ahead. And there is a wave of peace that comes with embracing the inevitable.

I always signed off on Facebook posts with "peace in your now" and since Peter died, I understand the *now* better than ever before. Maybe it's a lesson I can share with others. Maybe I can show, or tell, or be an example of how short life is and the only thing guaranteed is now.

So, be content in the most mundane, draw in your family while you're still whole, hold onto the magic feeling of Christmas because one day you may not care about the secrets it holds, and look for the happiness in the security of your life, even after a fight. And what if you did this all in the only time guaranteed? What if you did it *now*?

I Was Touched

I'm a low-maintenance kind of gal. I have never dyed my hair (aside from my 1980s 'Til Tuesday inspired rat's tail—that was a tail of many colors). I've chosen not to cover the gray coming in. I like my old people's highlights. I let my hair dry naturally, refusing a curler or a straightener. I've had three manicures in my life—two for friends' weddings and one for myself. I have only had two pedicures—one was a birthday gift. I can count on one hand how many professional massages I received in my life. My makeup is scarce and comes from pharmacies, as does my perfume when I wear it. The hotels I've stayed at have the numbers 8 or 6 in their names. I am great at finding deals on clothing, shoes, and purses. When it comes down to it, I'm Betsy from the Block. I am a low-maintenance, frugal, and some may say too lazy kind of gal. I am me.

Yesterday, I went to a hairstylist downtown Chicago and had a pedicure. I had made the hair appointment a day before, and I decided to get the pedicure as I passed by the salon. I've been craving physical touch, a connection to another human being.

I am a physically demonstrative person. I love to hug, kiss my friends and family, and even clasp hands with some friends when I talk. I like to hold and be held. I like a back rub, an arm around me, a soft touch to the cheek, or a messing up of my hair. I have boundaries, of course, but when it comes down to it, I like physical contact. I have always been that person.

Peter was good at doling out physical touch. He was physically affectionate without crossing any line or being obnoxious about it. He was a bit shy of public displays of affection except holding my hand, but when we were alone, he gave the best shoulder kneads, the greatest back rubs, and, oh my gosh, his scalp massages were to die for. And being me, I was greedy with my requests for any and all of the above. Now he and all of that are gone and I miss it. I miss it every day and curse Death for taking another thing away from me.

So, I decided to get my hair cut. I went online and just like that, I made an appointment. I went to the hair salon and the touching began. The washing of my hair, the cutting of it, not only relaxed me, but it also filled a small part of the whole missing. (One of the employees there asked me if I wanted a hand massage while the young man was cutting my hair. Like I was going to say no to that!)

As I exited the hair salon, relishing in the touches, I passed a nail salon next door. I made an impulsive decision to walk in and ask if there was availability. There was, and so began the pedicure. I'm a lot ticklish, so the pedicure itself wasn't very relaxing; I jerked back my feet a few times, almost kicking her face, and bit back the need to run away. Oh well. However, the massaging chair, the exfoliating of my calves and the little back rub afterward were heavenly.

Yesterday, the low-maintenance Betsy from the Block paid for a haircut and a pedicure. I put aside my thoughts of costs, frivolousness, and the feeling of selling out somehow. Peter is gone. His touches are phantom memories. I will never feel a caress from his large, callused hands with the just-right touch. I will never feel his awkwardly long arms wrapped around me, holding me, while I take in his scent, ever again. And no matter where I go or who I seek out, no one will ever be Peter. But for a while, yesterday, while my hair was getting cut and my feet pedicured, I was relaxed. A tiny section of me was filled, and I felt better, even for a bit. I'll take it. In the lousy world I live in without Peter, where good feelings are hard to come by, I'll take it.

Memories Hurt

I have a hard time with the memories of Peter. Not remembering them. I will never, nor could I ever, forget him and the memories we created. No, I struggle with cherishing the memories we created together, keeping them in my heart. I don't think I'm alone in this. There are many who find it torturous to hold the memories of their person after the person dies. Especially when it's brand new.

When I think of the last trip Peter and I went on, or a movie we laughed through, or a not-so-good dinner I shared with him, it hurts my heart. It hurts because the memories were created when Peter was alive. They are reminders of the times we spoke, laughed, touched, or were at peace together. And those times are gone. We will never be together again to form any more memories. That is what devastates me, every single time.

It used to be that when Facebook showed me a picture of a post about an event from a year or two back, I would sigh and smile and think, *That was a great time*. What used to be is gone, and now the memories pain me as I think, *That's when Peter was still alive*. It's my own fault, really. I posted too many gosh darn pictures and wrote too many words about me and "my mister"—the name I gave him and will never use again. I should have been more minimalist in my posts.

I can't really look at pictures of Peter either. I have one small photo of Peter in my bedroom at my apartment. The picture is of Peter and me when we first dated. I framed it and gave it to Peter when he left to work in Portland for six months. On the back of it, I wrote, "Whenever you're lonely, look at this picture and know how much I love you. Missing you, Betsy". Kind of prophetic, right? Yeah, that's why I keep it in my apartment. It's hard to look at—our young love just emerging. I don't find solace in it. Too many memories attached to a single picture. Perhaps one day.

I get why people tell me to cherish the memories. I probably said it to others in the past, too. There is a certain peace in remembering, and I admire the people who can find such peace, who even look for it. They're not afraid to look at the good. They may be stronger than I am, to be able to see past the pain to remember when life wasn't so painful. I want to know their secret or to capture their resolve. Perhaps one day I will, but for now, for today, on my own journey, it's not happening. I know love exists in the memories of Peter, Peter and me. I know it. I feel it every time I think of our time together, his smell, his touch, and his laugh. I feel the love and that pains me the most.

One day, I hope to look back and sigh. I hope to look at our memories as an acknowledgment of our strong love and feel a genuine need to think about them again. I hope to see Peter's lopsided grin, his salt and pepper hair, the lines creasing around his eyes when he smiled, and his slim body in a photograph and remember all we had together. I hope to conjure up memories of our trips, our movies, our dinners, and so much more without the pain I feel now when I remember. I hope I don't avoid looking at a picture of him, of us, because I don't want to remember what once was. I hope, one day, to see a memory on Facebook and think, *God, we loved each other hard and had what other people strive for—a complete and beautiful love affair.*

I hope, one day, I can cherish each and every memory of him, of us. But today is not that day. So for now, I just keep on going until I get to that day. I'll keep moving through the pain until my memories comfort me.

Grief Stopped Me

Yesterday, instead of fighting with grief, I succumbed to it. I rolled over and cried uncle. It was like grief threw up a stop sign, and I obeyed.

For the most part, I haven't stopped moving since Peter died. I haven't given up. I haven't stayed in bed balled up in anguish. I haven't let myself go. I haven't let anyone take care of or baby me. I would understand if a widow did any of these, and I probably would have done at least one of these if it weren't for the momentum of living for my kids and the hope of getting past the pain propelling me forward. Don't get me wrong. I have spent days standing still. There are some mornings where I stay in my pajamas and let the television suck me in. It doesn't feel great, but it doesn't feel bad. I give myself permission to succumb to powerlessness. Some days, when grief hits me and strikes me down, I stay down, like a boxer not wanting to get up again for another blow.

And, the other day, I texted friends to say I wasn't going to a party they invited me to. I just couldn't. I couldn't do the forty-plus minute drive back to my house. I couldn't sit in my puddle of grief while trying to look okay. I couldn't bring myself or my grief into a party because that wouldn't be fair to the festivities, to them. Still, I felt some guilt, even though I had been totally honest about myself to my friends. I mean, I do love these friends. I don't want to hurt them. Maybe I give myself too much credit for their feelings. In the end, I chose self-love and did what I thought was best at the moment.

Tennis pro Arthur Ash once said, "Start where you are, use what you have, do what you can." I'm not sure if he was talking about grief, but he described it well. I did what I needed to do. I started off feeling bad, I succumbed because that is all I had left in me, and I did what I felt was right for me. It helped me get through the day. It helped me feel what I had to feel. It helped me move forward.

I can't always be Superwoman, or Momentum Woman (a great name for a new DC character), or whoever else others perceive me to be. All I can be is me. And sometimes, it's okay for me to stop moving and roll over. It's okay because when I'm down there, I think of ways to help pull myself back up again. It gives me pause in my movement. When I move all the time, I don't always allow myself to feel, to come up with solutions, to do the things I might have to do in order to get through another day. And since Peter died, that's all I hope to do—move through another day. Move until I get to the point where I can actually live. And that will come. Even when I'm on the ground, I feel it coming. When I rise again, like this morning, I know it is there. Perhaps in the far distance, but I see it and I will get there. My momentum will take me there.

PART III

Look at Me Rise

This Golden Ring Doesn't Shine for Me Anymore

Sometimes it seems like a lifetime ago when Peter died. Other times it seems like yesterday. Most times it's some mixture of both. All the time, I know our life together is gone. I am no longer together with the one person who I created lives with, who became half of me, who I loved more than anyone I have ever known, and who was my person. I am without him forever and for always. I am a widow, his widow, and I move through life in a pain I have never known before.

There are moments in my day where I shake my head and think, *This really happened*. Then there are other times when disbelief does not exist, and perhaps those are the most painful. I know Peter is dead. I have never been in denial about it. From the moment the police officer came to my door, I knew Peter was gone, never to be part of me again. I can't seem to let go of the shock, the suddenness, and the unthinkable. I say to myself, to God, to Peter if he's listening, to the room, "*I cannot believe I will never see him ever again here on Earth or that our time together is over.*" I ask the question if I'll ever see him again.

Recently, I made a decision. It was something I had been thinking about for some time. Truth be told, it was a decision I knew from the beginning I would eventually make; it was only a question of when. I pulled the trigger, and I took off my wedding ring. It wasn't as if I woke up in the morning and said, "This is the day." I didn't do it ceremoniously or with fanfare. It was a day I met a friend for lunch, and the restaurant was across from the Jewelry District. I thought, *I need to get stones in another ring cleaned and tightened, and while I'm there . . .* I took my wedding ring from my left hand and placed it on my right. And it was done.

The ring I put on nearly twenty-eight years ago, the symbol of our marriage, our fidelity, our life together, no longer holds the same meaning now that Peter died. I am not married to Peter anymore. Death did us part. Oh, I feel love for Peter. I will always feel love for Peter. The love I feel for Peter is why grief, and all its pain, is still around. I can't, nor will I ever forget, the other half who created my children, and a huge part of me. But our marriage is now a once-was.

Taking off one's wedding ring is a very personal choice after a spouse dies. Many widows and widowers keep their wedding rings on for years. Others are buried with their rings on or take them off shortly after their spouse dies. My father was buried with his on, and my mother took her wedding ring off soon after he died. It wasn't because she loved him less than a widow who kept her wedding ring on for years. If you witnessed the way my mother took care of my father when he became really sick, you would have seen her love for him. It was a choice she made, and I never questioned it.

I thought of putting my ring on a chain with Peter's wedding ring. It's something a friend of mine did. But I play with necklaces and have broken my fair share of chains. I didn't want to break anything holding our rings and lose either or both of them. So I switched my wedding ring over to my right hand and placed Peter's on my middle finger, alongside it. It makes more sense for me there. I'm still reminded of our marriage, of his importance, of my passionate and deep consuming love for him. There may come a day I take off my ring altogether. Maybe not, though; I did wear it through pregnancies and childbirth, after all.

For some, it may seem quick to take off my wedding band. For others, it may seem like I held on too long. But for me, it was time. I've done everything on my own timeline since this all began. I have listened to my feelings and last week, I felt it was time. It was time for me to let go. Not of the man and the memories—I will forever hold onto both—but it was time to let go of the symbol of something we no longer can share: a life together.

Learning to Live Without Him

I had suicidal thoughts right after Peter died. My motherly instinct to be there for my kids gave me the strength to fight against those thoughts and the courage not to follow through. It also helped that three days after Peter died, I saw a therapist, and she helped me through this scary time. I encourage every widow and widower out there to seek help immediately, especially in the inherent pain right after your spouse dies. This is not something to handle alone. I couldn't do it alone. I had—I have—an amazing support system. And yet, at times, the death of a spouse is not something everyone can, or do, understand.

Society looks at widowhood as a "natural" end to a marriage. This expectation has been developed throughout history: Women's husbands died in battle, fighting for land or property, in hunting accidents, and/or from illnesses. Men have always died earlier than women, especially once childbirth was no longer as threatening to women's health. A husband's death was expected. When wives died, men were expected to marry again, quickly, for the purposes of child-rearing and homemaking. Losing a wife was never talked about among men. And it's still not. Men notoriously do not have the same type of support system women have, and they are less likely to seek out help. Widowhood was the way of the world. Thus, widows were allowed to grieve for a bit, then told to shrug it off and move on. I think there is still a little bit of this effect from years past. I don't think people want to talk about widowhood, maybe because it's difficult to imagine in their own lives, or it has not happened.

A death of a spouse is a pain no one understands until it happens. It's like breaking a leg. You don't really know what it feels like until it happens to you. Of course, there is the compassion and sympathy given by most, but there is also the underlying admission of, "*I'm sorry, but I don't understand*" that only the grieving can understand. After a certain point, people move on with their lives, but the widow(er) does not. The spouseless person is still without their person.

The other day I listened to an interview with a country singer. He spoke about his son who died a few years earlier and the pain he still feels. He told a story of a friend he had not seen since his son's death who said, "Wow, I can't believe it's been years." The singer responded that it's "every day" for him.

The pain of a spouse's death stays with you every day. You feel it in the couple ahead of you in a movie line holding hands. You think about it in your financial decisions. You hear it in the phone calls asking for your dead spouse or see it a piece of mail addressed to him. It stays with you through the holidays, birthdays, and anniversaries. You experience it in the memories of the streets you walked down together, the houses you drove past. Loss, longing, and grief are the constants in every part of the survivor's life, but not in the part of the person observing. It's hard to continually pour out empathy without experience, to keep up with the fading of time.

There are fronts we widows and widowers put forth and roles we play. We don't like being miserable all the time. We can remember how effortless it was to be happy, and we want to get there again. We don't want to accept our lives will never be the same, that we'll never feel the same. So we fake it. In the process, we fool people, even those closest to us, into believing we have moved on. With a sigh of relief, those people feel they can move on as well. They don't understand that we're faking it 'til we make it, yet we never make it, there or anywhere. We exhaust ourselves in pretending. At the end of the day, when it's only you—because the other part of you is gone and you sit in the reality of your feelings—the pain comes. Sometimes it comes like little needles puncturing parts of your heart. Sometimes it comes in an avalanche of spears piercing you. Either way, it comes. It doesn't know there is a deadline, a timeline, a stopping point that we think it should have.

I am so much better. I laugh more. My humor, my sarcastic, odd humor is coming back in small quips, one at a time. I am again writing romance, even with my muse gone. Memories of Peter are welcomed in now, even encouraged. I am learning and growing and moving. I have held onto those who stayed with me, are staying with me, and am slowly releasing my expectations of others who disappointed me. I am trying to forgive. I am learning to live without him, like other widows have told me I would. Most importantly, suicidal thoughts are not crowding me; they do not even come. I still hurt. I still feel the pain of his loss. I still miss him, every day. God, I miss him.

It All Flu In

Being sick is its own kind of loneliness, especially at night. When darkness invades your bedroom and it's just you, alone and muddled with fever and an upset stomach. You lie in a state of confusion brought on by a high temperature and battles of nausea that attack your body in unsuspecting waves. You are the only one to take care of yourself, while you toss and turn, praying for relief, and you hope daylight comes to bring relief. When you are living alone, your solitude comes at you in quick, harsh reminders. The grief you carry with you since Death opened up a wormhole to another life you thought never possible, is heavier and more burdensome than it is in the times you are well.

Alone, you roll out of bed to do laundry, change sheets, and clean up the mess the flu made while your fever climbs, and you tell yourself, *I can't do this . . .* only to respond, *You have to.* And after your body is spent, the flu having done all it could, your exhaustion traps you into an almost vegetative state, and you lie with yourself in your own ache. At three o'clock in the morning, you can no longer call out to the person you once called out to.

Even when dawn breaks through and the bug is still not done with its attack, the idea of reaching out to someone is too fatiguing, and you wish (as you wish every day but this time even more) your person was back so he could walk in, sit down, and put a cool hand on your forehead like he once did. You wish for comfort and compassion and sympathy without asking for it. You wish the stomach bug never came during your grief, for together, they made you feel an emptiness you have never felt in your life.

Tears don't come. Maybe dehydration makes it impossible, or maybe it's knowing the futility of them. In their place comes a deep sadness, the one you have had since he died but is pushed down so you can function in life. Now it comes up strong, like the bile you just spewed, and you lie with it, knowing it is your reality. And when you call out to him, asking him just to come back, just this one time when you need him, not knowing if it is the fever or desperate loneliness taking over your thoughts, an answer comes in with a clarity you haven't had since the bug came. You know coming back is not an option, never an option, and it is all on you. Everything now, every decision, every choice, every emotion, every illness, cannot be shared with him anymore. He can no long offer relief. This is your new reality. This stomach bug showed you this answer, an answer survival didn't want to share, as you toss yet again and turn once more.

When the bug's time is up and leaves you with aftershocks of depletion and fragility, you begin to cry. You cry for your victory. You cry for relief of the bug's retreat. You cry for the all the loneliness, and the despair, and the longing. You cry from the texts of concerns and questions of "*What can I do to help?*" You cry because the uncertainty of whether anyone cared was eased. And you cry because this flu has also taken you toward a different path on this reluctant journey, a path of reality, determination, and an awareness you can survive life's best shots. This flu gave you a new kind of sadness you have to tackle, and now you know, truly know, you can carry on in its aftermath. You have survived.

And then, you pick up the phone to call and text the people who are still living in your life and who care for you. And you have a gratitude for them, unlike one you have ever known before. And in the midst of your thoughts of *wow, that was horrible* and *that was the loneliest flu I ever had*, you kind of smile—a sad, strangled smile, but you do smile. You pick up your weary body and ask life, "What next?"

I Wish, Part 2

I wish I didn't have to see couples, especially aging couples. They remind me of what will never be but I still want to be. Their comfortable silence, their laughter at inside jokes built on years of togetherness, their squeezes of hands, and the worry wrinkling on their faces when the other one struggles to walk all remind me growing old with Peter will never happen. What I thought, what I took for granted, what I always assumed, just won't.

I wish I didn't see social media posts about and see pictures of couples for the same reasons above. I know, most of my posts in the past were about Peter and me. And I know none of them will ever be again.

I wish I didn't have to travel alone. Being in a car with an empty space next to me serves as a blaring reminder of my solo act and makes it difficult to see the road through tear-stung eyes.

I wish I didn't have to sleep by myself. Not hearing Peter's wall-shaking snores is the most deafening silence I know.

I wish songs didn't remind me so much of him and bring out the emotions I try so hard to tuck inside of me.

I wish I cared more for what was going on with the world, in the US, instead of being so damn wrapped up in my own (and my children's) emotions, sadness, grief. Once upon a time, I would have commented on the goings-on of the election, politics, even sports; instead, I don't even realize March Madness is starting, or that the primaries are around the corner. I can't right now.

I wish I was not such a one-dimensional friend, always bringing it back to me and my longing for Peter. Instead of the confusing (because I am more than confused) or the self-centered (because pain has taken center stage in my life) conversations, I could engage with friends, maybe even spark conversations, and keep my focus on them. But I can't do that either. And I hate this part of grief the most. More and more lately, I feel my friends are tiring of me. They don't even seem to know what to say or do anymore, so they stop, or lessen. I feel it, and I can't say I blame them.

I wish grief wouldn't tease me, making me feel okay one minute and then so sad the next. Consistency would be nice.

I wish my head and my heart would be in sync. My mind knows what to do, or what it should do, and my broken heart just can't follow. Once, they agreed. Now, they battle, leaving me confused and indecisive.

I wish everything was not on me because the partnership, my partnership with a kind, gentle man, was killed off.

I wish, damn it, I wish Peter didn't die and he was still here with me and I was whole again. I was able to move and feel and engage once, instead of the awkward, shaky movements I make as I move, ill-prepared, in this life without Peter.

Finally, I wish to one day look back on all of this and say, "I've learned to live with you, Grief, and I am stronger because I did." And then, things, emotions, my life will have begun to fall into a semblance of order. No, this is not just a wish. This is my goal.

She Remembers Him

My mother sat there, her shock of grey hair peeping out
from the back of the wheelchair which has now become
part of her being. I maneuvered my way to her back table,
smiling at the other residents and saying passing *I know*'s
to the staff who commented on my strong resemblance to
her. Their observations are a source of pride as I think of
her, still, as this beautiful woman I have hero-worshipped
all my life.

"Hi, Mom," I said as I bent down to hug her body,
smaller than her once strong and solid frame.

"Hi," she responded with an ignited light in her eyes.
"I'm so happy to see you. Your in-laws were just here."

"My in-laws?" I asked and pulled back my head in
surprise. "Really?"

"Yes," she said with a smile, the gentle, warm smile I
have known since youth. "Peter's mother and father. They
stopped in and said they were on their way to . . ." She
names the small town my husband grew up in near central
Illinois.

My in-laws have been dead for quite some time. I
barely knew Peter's father. He died a year before we were
married. And his mother, my gentle and beautiful mother-
in-law, died over ten years ago. During my private moment
with Peter's lifeless body at the hospital, I said aloud to

him, "I hope your parents greeted you first." He loved his
parents, especially his mother. To have them with him in
the afterlife —a belief I still hold onto from my youth—
was a comfort to me; it still is.

"Well," I said, learning to roll with my mother's state,
"I hope you had a good time."

"We did. We did." She got a faraway look in her eye
recapping her imaginary visit. "They're such nice people."

I sat down and we had a jumbled conversation of
what she believed to be true. She grew agitated at one
point and asked me to make sure the FBI had coffee when
they came next time. What FBI? When did they come? I
didn't know because it was part of her confused world. I
spent time reassuring her it would get done. She calmed
and then asked how "her girl" was doing. Her girl was
my daughter's dog, Lily, who comes to visit with my
daughter when she's in. My mother's smile grew with the
recollection of Lily, and for the next few minutes, our
discussion centered around the dog and all her antics,
which made my mother laugh. As quickly as she retreated
from her own world, she returned with the insistence of
completing her FBI request. Again, I promised I would see
what I could do.

With her a little calmer now, she ate her lunch, her
gaze focused out the window ahead of her. I stared at her,
wondering what was in her head, where she had drifted off
to, and when she would let go of the agitation she held as
she struggled with reality. We sat like this, in the silence of
our own thoughts, for long beats. After a time, she looked
and asked me what the "little guys" were saying now. Not

certain if she meant my kids, now in their early twenties, or her great grandchildren. When I asked for clarification, she just smiled and said yes. I assumed she meant her great grandchildren, so I gave her some anecdotes of what I knew from the last time I saw them, one more recently than the other. She followed for a while until her gaze and thoughts drifted out the window again.

As she shoveled in one more mouthful of her food and then pushed the plate away, my mother asked, "And how are Betsy and Peter?" I didn't correct her. I stopped correcting my mother with reminders of Peter's death a while ago. It didn't matter, and really, she didn't have to know. So I nodded and said they were doing fine. She smiled and picked up her coffee cup with shaky hands and took a sip from it. "Your farmer boy is doing fine, then?" She had come to refer to Peter as my "farmer boy." I nodded yes.

When she leaned forward to put down her cup, I rubbed her back. Her eyes hooded, and she cooed out, "That feels good." I said I was glad and continued doing it. When she told me that I didn't have to keep doing it, I asked if she wanted me to stop and she whispered, "No, please don't." And, so, for the next few minutes, I rubbed my mother's back like she did to me when I needed to be comforted, when I needed to be settled down from an all-confusing world.

I left a little over an hour after I got there. Before I did, I kissed her forehead and smiled down at her. I told her I loved her, and she said, "Yeah, but can you see if . . ." and her concern went back to the FBI of her muddled world. I told her, "Sure, Mom. I'll get it done."

On the drive home, thoughts exploded in my head, and the shrapnel landed in my heart. My mother was not there anymore. She occasionally has good days, but for the most part, age has taken her from me. My hero has been taken at a time I needed her to put on her superwoman cape for me, and I mourn her. And although she left me, I know I now have someone for whom I can do my best to reciprocate the comfort and reassurance she gave me during my lifetime. Only, sometimes it's too hard.

Every time I see her, it's hard. Not only because I see the absence of the strong, brilliant, example of a woman, of a mother, but because it reminds me, all the time, how unfair life is, Death is. Peter died an extremely healthy man while my mother remains in a shell she doesn't want to be in anymore. How fair is this? And this is the reason why my two-a-week visits to her have been chiseled down to once every two weeks, sometimes longer. And why guilt crashes into me, causing me more pain and agony. I want to see her more, yet grief holds me back.

As I get onto another expressway, I smile, which turns into a laugh. My mother's mind may be jumbled at times, yet she is clear on two things. One, she remembers, always remembers Lily and those positive emotions a dog can bring. And two, she never forgets Peter. Whether it be "your farmer boy" or "Betsy and Peter," she remembers him and she does because she loved him, she loves him. And I think, how great that I married and lived with a man my mother approved of so much, she still has a part in her mind just for him. It is then that I gain some peace.

Dancing in the Fog

Widow's fog is a real thing when a spouse dies. From what I understand, there's a part of the brain, the prefrontal cortex, used to understand, memorize, recall, and deal with complex issues. This part of the brain is compromised when death occurs, especially the death of a spouse. After a death, because that part of the brain is accustomed to handling one thing at a time, it is exhausted by the flood of decisions, memories, and emotions. The person who normally helped those processes—recalled, created memories, and assisted in understanding—is gone. So, a fog, a widow's fog, descends and blocks out the normal process.

The best way I can describe widow's fog, or widow's brain, is like walking around with a head cold. You want to focus. You really want to remember. You know you have to organize. And yet, the heaviness of the head cold, resting on your shoulders like a block of cement, makes it impossible as focus is gone. The only thing you feel is exhausted and frustrated.

I have made, then changed, then made decisions. I avoided decisions. I tend to ramble, especially in texts and emails, as I try to organize my thoughts to make my point. My disorganization that has always been with me is worsened. And because of all of these struggles, this massive effort to focus, I walk around exhausted, all the time. Throw in a mind like mine, my all-over-the-place mind, and my widow's fog is frightening.

I like my brain. I do. I like how it takes me from point A to point E in less than six seconds. I like the thoughts that pop up in it, thoughts most probably don't even think about or wonder about. I like my mind's deep thoughts, my mind's funny thoughts, my mind's trivial thoughts that all seem to arrive at once. It's how I have always rolled, and it fuels my creative side. However, now, as Widow's Fog descends on me, on my mind, I am tired, and I struggle.

I get embarrassed by my forgetfulness and the *yeah-not-sure-where-I-put-that* moments. I cringe at the number of times I change my mind. I am angered when I can't decide. My brain I once celebrated, I am now angry at. I know this doesn't help it, doesn't help me, doesn't help anything.

I am learning to accept the normality of my widow's fog and its effects on my brain right now because it doesn't seem to be going away. It takes time, especially since Peter was the one who made most decisions, who was the person to take over when I faltered, who had a love language of doing without me asking, and who was the person to center me. I no longer have Peter in my life to depend on, or lean on, or step in. I am missing my rock I had to balance on, to support me, to hold me up.

I am trying to be patient with myself and my brain, knowing eventually my mind will return to whatever normal is for me. I am attempting to embrace the head cold feeling and rest when I need it. I am convincing myself it's okay to change my mind, put off some decisions. I am getting less embarrassed in explaining to my friends and my kids that it's not them, it's me, and hoping they understand. I am giving my all to organization, something I never had, but I am finding it more helpful when I do. Eventually, I will see the light in the fog. I will see a clearing to the other side.

As I stand on my own, I'm a bit wobbly, a bit nervous. I'm so out of practice, and I am totally overwhelmed. But I am standing. I am standing in this fog that surrounds me, trying to get my bearings in its murk. I am taking steps through it despite my indecisiveness, my forgetfulness, and my disorganization. And, when I finally get to the light of my new normalcy, I will dance the most beautiful dance with Victory, while grief watches from the sidelines. Until then, I'll just keep moving through the fog.

In the Darkness, He Came to Me

I went to bed early last night and in tears. I wanted, no *needed*, to put the day to rest. I awoke in the middle of the night, only to drift back to the point where my mind and body were melting into a dreamlike state but not yet there. In that state, I felt a shift in my bed, the kind of roll you feel when someone has joined you. Then, there was a wave of warm, caressing chills over me while goosebumps exploded on the back of my neck and on my hairline. Both were peaceful and comforting, yet a bit frightening too. When I sensed soft kisses on my lips, I relaxed for a bit, until the fear jolted me. I did not want to open my eyes, but when I did, my heart raced with conflicting feelings of fear and peace from feeling Peter next to me. This happened twice again to me that night. Each time when I floated back to sleep, I felt him, except without the shifting in bed, except with the absence of a kisses.

Let me say this. All three times, I know I was not sleeping, but I wasn't awake either. Sometimes, at night, as I lie in bed, I close my eyes and give into the darkness I see behind my lids. I allow myself to be carried into it, as deep as I am able to go until fear of the unknown jerks me out of it. But while I'm "there," everything else around me doesn't exist—sound, touch, a sense of presence. It's just me and the darkness. I think some would describe it as meditation. I'm not sure, as I never thought of myself as a person who meditates. Whatever state it is, this happened to me three times last night. I didn't feel like I was on a bed in a room, rather like I was existing in a space of nonthreatening, unafraid darkness.

I can break this down and try to analyze it logically. These three incidents may have happened at a time I missed Peter so much that my subconscious gave me him. Or perhaps it was all a dream, the same dream three times. It happens. I've had a recurring dream of my parents in their bedroom eating pound cake. (Don't ask.) Or maybe my brain tricked me into believing any of this in an attempt to move on in grief. These all make sense to my brain, yet to my heart, the one thing that has ruled me since birth, it just doesn't.

I know I have a strong imagination. My invisible friend from my childhood, J.J., could attest to that. I believe imagination is a way to open your mind to other possibilities. Maybe this openness allows me to experience these possibilities. Grief is so unknown and different for everyone, so maybe it works on a part of my brain I never had to use before, giving me glimpses into the unexplored. Maybe there is a part of my heart that loves Peter so strongly, it called out to him and he responded. Or maybe it doesn't even matter if it was real or not.

Maybe all that does matter is that for a moment, for those moments, I felt the deep connection that only existed in the tangible world and now can no longer be. Maybe all that matters is in the morning when I awoke, I felt Peter was with me, in one form or another, and it gave me comfort. While a new me emerges with severed parts of Peter, I know he will always be part of what I was, who I am now, and what I will become.

I'm not going to think too hard on the *why's* or the *if's*. I won't examine the craziness this sounds like to some, or how others see it as desperation grief gave me. I won't even defend myself and what I knew to be real. All I will do is sit with it and smile and think, *Peter came to me in the darkness.* And that will be enough.

Mumzy, Go Gentle into Your Visit

"Come here for a second." She crooked her arthritic finger at me, so I walked over to her. She looked up at me with her once deep brown eyes, but now covered in grey cataracts, and said, "Pray to Peter and ask him how I can visit him in heaven."

These were my mother's last words to me. Yesterday, the woman I honored, hero-worshipped, respected, liked and loved all my life, the woman I called Mumzy, went to start her eternal visit with Peter, as she passed peacefully.

My mother was a month away from ninety-two when she died. A long life for a woman with strong heart, stronger soul, and a peaceful, gentle beauty about her. For the past few years, she's wanted to die. She believed in the afterlife and wanted to join her husband, family members, and friends who have passed before her. Toward the end of her life, her once brilliant mind was riddled with dementia and not the life meant for her.

There is so much I can tell you about my mother. She had an amazing biography that included living through the Great Depression, multiple wars, civil unrest, 9/11, and numerous viruses. She was a class or two shy of a college diploma, a rarity for a woman of ninety-two. She had seven children in eleven years with three miscarriages and nursed my (always sick-to-me) father until his death.

She worked full-time, another part of her uniqueness in a time when *June Cleaver* and *Carol Brady* reigned. She climbed as high as she could in the accounting department of a manufacturing firm. She was not only a union representative there, but also the first woman to hold an executive position on the union board.

As my mother, she showed me what dedication to your spouse looked like. She served as an example of holding a large family together. She said to me once, "I am glad none of my kids ended up in jail." Not only are we jail-free, but we were also educated, and bathed and fed and housed and, most importantly, loved. Yes, she made mistakes. As a mother myself, I know motherhood is not perfection. Mothers always do the best they can with what they have and maybe better than what they had. My mother did just that . . . and then some.

My mother and Peter had a mutual love for each other, and perhaps it was because of their similar strengths. Their gentle kindness, their quiet, unassuming ways, their priority of family including sacrifices, and their brilliant brains were just some of the same qualities that others respected in them. I never married a man like my father. I married a man like my mother.

As of yesterday, two of the people who I treasured most, who took the greatest care of me in my life, have died. Death, once again, took someone away from me, and I am shattered from the loss of her. I know she has gone to visit Peter like she wanted, and for that, I am moved.

I am here, left behind, trying to conjure up the strength I have never used, but one I can look to my mother and try to emulate. I am her daughter. Goodbye, Mumzy. My already torn heart rips more today with the pain of losing you, my hero. Tell Peter I said hi, and I really hope you have a nice visit with him.

Nine Months

Nine months ago, when Death knocked me on my ass and took Peter from my life, I became a widow. It's not really an anniversary, is it? Anniversaries are for celebrating, and hell, if I'll ever celebrate Peter's death. I suppose it's more of a marker point, an indication how long I have lived without Peter, and today it's been nine months.

Peter's death left me damaged and halved. I am no longer the person I once was, nor will I ever be again. I have lived in the hell I was pushed into by Peter's killing, and still, on my bad days, I live in its heat, trying to understand it all. Even after nine months have passed, I still live in shock. It may not be as often, and that's a good thing, yet I still scream at God, the Universe, *why* and *how could you*. My faith has not returned to what it once was, but I am working on it, and that's all I can do, as exhausting as it is most days. Everything is different now and I feel no comfort or pride in my forced changes.

Nine months ago, my life shattered, and I am still picking up each broken piece. Some I throw away, some of the ones I had with Peter, the ones I no longer need. Others, the ones that are me to my core, I try to place back, and like a jigsaw piece you try to force in the wrong place, some don't fit. Not without Peter, they won't fit.

Peter was so much a part of my core. Nine months later, I am growing new pieces, and it can be uncomfortable and torturous. They can also look good, good enough where I say aloud, "Look at me."

Today serves as a reminder of the day Peter died. Today, I will be angry Peter was taken way too soon. Today, I will try to grapple with the nonexistent reasons as to why he is gone. Today, I will carry the knot in my stomach which formed nine months ago and weep in hopes of lessening its strength. Today, I will try to see all my growth and strength, because both are there, and reflect back on how far I've come. Today, I will remember Peter and his crooked smiles, his quiet voice, his gentle touches, his reassurances, and his joys in life. Today, I will remember how he lived life to its fullest, doing what he loved, even if this means knowing Death ripped him away from me doing just that. And today, between the tears, maybe even through them, I will smile, for he was mine and I was his, until Death did part us, nine months ago today.

Grief in the Times of COVID

The world doesn't stop for my grief. It shouldn't. Especially in this time of a pandemic, my grief should not matter. And I hope it doesn't to anyone but me. The deaths of Peter and my mom added an extra layer of loneliness and foreboding to this time where we are all lonely and everything feels foreboding. We are all staring down a virus so strong, it threatens us all. I understand the terror of this virus. I know we are all in this together. I know we are all scared, longing to hug again, to go out for lunch, see a movie and rid ourselves of our required wardrobe change, the mask. We are all seeking some type of return to our normalcy. I know all of this, and feel all of this, yet I still carry my own grief.

Grief is a selfish beast, and I have been caught in its claws. I don't want to be. I would love to wave some magic wand over me and tell it to be gone. But I can't, and I still am being ripped by grief's talons. The tears I have in my eyes, the tears there from the loss of significant people, make it too difficult to see others sometimes. Not all the time, but sometimes.

This pandemic has given us all time of reflection. It has slowed us down, made us all turn inward, perhaps examine our lives. The silence has made our thoughts louder. And this means my thoughts are shouting in my own loneliness made more intense by my grief. I sit in a house all day, surrounded in memories of him, of us, of what was. Any room I walk into, anything I see, serves as a reminder of Peter. And while my memories of Peter are starting to bring on smiles, finally, they also serve as what is missing in me, in my life. Because, hell, I loved him. I want him, especially in this lonely time of COVID.

Now, I could escape. I could run away to my apartment in the city and run the risk of getting sick there or having to quarantine there. Don't think I haven't thought about it many times. Yet I stay put. My son is here, near me in my suburban home, and he has brought me groceries and made me dinner. He has heard my ramblings. He is here, and I am here for him. There is a comfort in knowing I have him and the neighbors I love, some for over twenty years, here for me and I for them if needed. Plus, to be honest, my apartment may not hold all the memories, yet there would still be a sense of missing Peter and my mom. Getting away is not an answer as long as the distractions are few in the imprisonment of this pandemic.

During COVID, I feel selfish. I feel I should "get over it" or "move on" because we are all looking down the same barrel of the pandemic gun which can be pulled at any time and blow any of us, any of our loved ones, away. I feel people are struggling and my grief means nothing anymore, or perhaps less, or perhaps needs to be shut down, not talked about. I feel I should shout at my grief, at myself, *Shut up already because this pandemic is bigger than you and your grief.* And it is. And I can't.

COVID has stagnated me and my grief. I am still on a road to healing. I cry fewer tears, experience more laughter, and some days, I even feel less of a need to share. I am getting used to living with my broken heart. Then there are these days, these moments, when I see a picture of Peter, hear a song to remind me of him, or feel the memories we made in the house we loved, the house I am forced to stay in, and I am slapped back down in grief without an outlet to distract me. And I hate these days of lockdown more than anyone else. I wish they were gone, but wishes don't always come true, do they?

I know, we are in this pandemic together. Some are working on the frontline of it. Some are stocking grocery shelves, delivering, and trying to do their part for essential businesses. Some are teaching in a new way. Some are learning a new way. Some are trying to keep their businesses afloat. Some of us are grieving in it. All of us are carrying around our own burdens of varying degrees. All of us know someone who has it worse or better or different than us and appreciate what we have. All of us know the heroes in this and appreciate what they sacrifice. All of us are in this together as the world goes on. And I go on in it, for better or worse, with my grief. Damn it.

Forgetting I Am Alone

Sometimes I forget I am alone. Not often, and when I do, the moment goes by so fast it may have beaten a wink. Still, I do . . . forget that I am alone.

But most times, I don't forget at all. Most times, I carry loneliness with me like old skin ready to be shed, only I know the impossibility of it, for right now, because Peter is gone, and he was the one who filled me up. He was the one I always knew would be there for me no matter how my friends left or how rough my day was. He was that reliable person for me, on a rough day or in times when I felt no one could hear me, on those lonely days filled with missed turns and hurt, he would be there, always. But our always was cut too short, too soon, without notice, leaving me reeling in fear of the loneliness without him.

Yesterday, on a walk with my dog, I thought of all life handed me—surgeries, concussions, a few cancer scares, getting hit by a car as a pedestrian, and the loss of jobs I loved. I remembered when all of these things happened in the span of three years, I had Peter, and now I don't. His death was the cherry on the top of my this-doesn't-happen-to-anyone-but-me recent life. Thinking this, I turned in the direction of self-pity, spiraling down with thoughts of when life will become kind to me again. And aloneness hit me hard, reeling me back from the reality of it all, from the pain of it all, from the fear of it all.

Last night, I had a huge crying jag, admitting to a friend my fear of the future and how that would look. Where do I go from here? How do I face the solitude of the years ahead, or the quiet of my life? I know it is inevitable, so how do I handle it? What will my life look like now without Peter? I am still a new widow, yet I'm getting further away from the beginning of it and looking into the forever of it. Maybe it's a sign of healing or growing pains. Or maybe it's just another stage I have to enter, one I am gripping onto the door frame trying to prevent entrance.

As a new widow, I had to deal with just staying afloat. I'm bobbing now and I have no idea where to paddle to, and I'm overcome with the fear of doing it all alone. Being alone will continue to shadow me with some days darker than others. And the only reliance I have is on myself. I can't and won't, depend on anyone else. It's me I have to answer to, my life I have to live, my Peter who died in sudden shock.

I was pissed off yesterday and last night when thoughts of my loneliness pushed me back, not necessarily to grief, but fear. *What-if's* and the future kept scratching at the panic in me with their long, unforgivable talons of reality. What if I fail without Peter? What if I continue to be numb to everything as a defense in order to survive? What if I am forgotten, by friends, by family, by me, the once-me? What if I lose people along the way because who I become is not what they liked in who I once was? And what if my fear of disloyalty to his memory prevents me from liking the person I become without him?

Lately, I felt strength emerging from me. I wrote more of my novel. I rescued another mutt, Barkley, that I didn't have a reaction to, and started walking three miles a day with him. I began to clean out the house and get it ready to sell. I purged the old clothes from the summer before with all its memories to make room for new clothes for the future. I started eating better, more conscious of what should be going in my body. I took an honest look at the amount of wine consumed to dull the pain. I looked toward a future and better me in the process. And then life threw back its head and said to me, "If only it was that easy." I answered back, self-pity biting at each word, "You're right, because easy hasn't been a part of my life for a while." And I remembered I am without Peter, and I felt alone.

Most times lately, especially in my future-thinking moments, I have these nanoseconds of forgetting I am alone in this. There are times when my aloneness tries to take me down a road of fear and pity. And yes, everything will eventually merge onto one road, or so everyone who knows widowhood tells me. Still, during those times I take those detours, I hurt like hell, and I am afraid.

It Came For Me

It came at me again tonight. It snuck up on me like some unwanted slithering snake, sliding over me until it wrapped around my soul to choke it. It was my own fault. I was growing complacent. I grew cocky in thinking grief had lessened to a manageable existence. Besides, the world has turned upside down these past months with COVID, lessening my grief in order to face the hard times ahead. And yet, tonight, my grief rushed by the virus to show me its presence, and I sobbed.

The pandemic pushed back grief. I didn't want to be so egocentric when the world was so much bigger than me. Most people don't want to hear about it now while in their own pains and feeling their own frustration. So my grief laid untouched, not just by others, but by me too, and things not handled are forgotten. The virus in front of it, blocking grief's view, its feel, its importance. Only, it was still there, no matter where it was placed. Grief never lost its footing in my life. I lost my vision of it, but it was still there.

Even as my grief lessens or becomes more comfortable in me, it still surrounds me, picking at the scab it formed in my being. And tonight, the scab was scratched opened by a memory, and I bled out again. The pain, the unfairness of it all, the inability to understand, the anger, the despair, the longing—oh God, the longing—all spurted out of the veins in my heart that held him. I hate it, again. And I wish it would go back behind the sheet the virus holds up to hide it from me.

But wishes don't come true and this one was no exception. It came through. All the pains of missing him came out of me, along with the agony, the self-pity of living without him, the screams of agony to God, The Universe, trying to understand when I am going to get a fucking break from life. Trying to grasp why this prickly tag of *"grieving widow"* keeps rubbing me when I move toward a life without Peter. Like when I try to live as a writer and see the poor sales numbers of my latest book, I fear my writing is going nowhere, so I fall back in defeat, cussing at life for the punches I keep on receiving. And my guilt reminds me of the people who are sick, dying, and losing jobs, and I succumb to more pain.

I fooled myself. I always knew grief never left me. It couldn't when all its causes remain. I am still a widow. I am still widowed from a man who I knew for thirty-two years and fathered my children. I am still a widow who did not choose this, ask for it, or see it coming. It whooshed into my life and I spun from its force for months. But then I slowed, until I didn't, until grief reminded me it is still a powerful force in my life. I thought I steadied myself, but it came through again, knocking me off-balance. And, for tonight, I wish I could be just another person in this world, living my life as part of this scary pandemic. Instead, I am a widow, Peter's widow, *and* living in a scary pandemic. And it is too much. So, I cry.

I will put this day to bed with a goodnight now, knowing tomorrow holds promises and new beginnings. I believe in tomorrow because of the good that came out of past tomorrows. Yes tonight, grief came at me, again, reminding me it's not done with me, and maybe I shouldn't push too hard to be done with it.

Growing in the Pain

As I grow as a person without my spouse, my grief has stretched my emotions to levels I have never felt before. The agony is inside my soul, a place never touched so deeply before, and it spreads throughout, banging on my heart, my head, in my belly. It renders me useless for a time as I collapse into guttural sobs, asking God, the Universe, why. The answer of, *"There is no answer,"* does not give me any comfort, yet I know it's the only one. It amazes me how one minute, one hour, one day, I can be okay, even good, then the next minute or hour or day, I can be completely destroyed. Grief lulls me into a deceptive feeling of semi-normalcy, only to shake me up with its brutality, scattering me everywhere. And yet, I continue on, as a widowed person.

I started to release anger toward Peter. I started to let go of the frustration of the things left for me to deal with. I began practicing my goodbye speeches to resentments and unfulfilled moments and those pesky, recurring arguments never resolved. I opened a window to show all of my negative fury an escape.

I know anger is part of grieving. It's necessary, or so I'm told. I understand that because now I understand anger is controlled sadness. God knows, since Peter died, I have had so much sadness. Anger had me look at the entirety of my marriage, our marriage, which included seeing the not so nice things. Marriage is not perfection. In understanding the totality of my marriage, I faced my perceived imperfections of him, of me, of us in our marriage. As I reflected on and accepted all of this, I have started to see anger as a hindrance, not a help, a place I need to free up to receive all that was good in Peter, in us.

I have held onto a lot of anger toward Peter, anger I don't share with other people. For as raw and honest as I am in life, I am also aware of how much words can hurt. I do not want to hurt my children or his family by sharing grievances and anger about a father, a sibling they love. It's not my right to spew negatively about another based on my perception and experiences. Besides, now, looking back, maybe even during, I know some of the anger was misplaced, and for a lack of a better word, stupid. Part of the anger stemmed from recurring issues never resolved, as happens in long marriages. Anyway, it doesn't matter now, because I am starting to let it go and may be starting to move past the anger stage of grieving. I'm just at the beginning, but at least I'm in the wings.

Anger has been easy to feel. It takes away some of the pain of moving on, maybe the guilt. But by doing this, it begs the question of who really grows in anger? My mom once told me after I threw a tantrum that rivaled a two-year-old the night before I moved out on my own, it's easier to move away when you're angry. It's harder to move on when you are good, even happy.

I think about the good in Peter, in us as a couple. I think how the two of us believed and valued the same things. I think how mutual decisions made in all our years together were to benefit the family because the family was our priority above all else. I think about how our similar backgrounds steadied us and gave us our understanding of each other. I think how I appreciated my attraction to him, my draw to him, what kept me to him. It was not just the physical—although he was sexy as hell—but I realized we belonged together. We were meant to be together on a level so deep I am still trying to unravel it all. These thoughts are what begins to slowly release some of my built-up anger, and the release is agonizing.

See, pushing past the anger to see the good is an indescribable agony understood by those who have faced the same challenge. Anger will hold you in place one way or another. As long as you have anger, you hold onto whatever is left. Releasing the anger means you are forced to face all the good, all of what you loved in the past tense, and that fucking hurts.

I grew a lot last week. I grew because I embraced all of what Peter was to me, all that we had together. And it was good. It was strong. It was loving. It was right. And embracing it was painful, for I knew, with every embrace, there comes a time to let go. And while it felt so good to weaken my anger and let in the beauty of Peter and our lives together, I also started to understand the finality of it all. It sent me into a two-day depressed state, one I still am hungover from. These growing pains are hard, and I am a little pissed off by them.

A Walk by the Wetlands With Peter

I took my dog, Barkley, for a walk. I got Barkley a few weeks after my mom died and he has turned out to be a great companion. Anyway, we walked together on the path by the wetlands in the back of my house. The place holds so many memories for me. It was the shortcut to the school my children attended, the path he helped build, the prairie he helped maintain, the fields my daughter played baseball in for two seasons, and open areas our dogs would run in. It was the time I spent with Peter on breezy spring nights, hot summer days, and crisp fall mornings, holding hands as we walked with birds flying overhead, frogs croaking love songs, or snow swirling around us. It was there where problems were solved, the state of the world was addressed, and we simply walked in the comfortable quiet I knew so well with Peter.

The hour after his memorial service, family and friends walked with my kids and me around the path as a final goodbye to Peter. It is where, later, his ashes were scattered, among the land he so loved. I feel close to him on these wetlands. I hear our memories come alive and feel his presence among it all. So, I walk there at least four times per week. I'll talk to Peter when I'm there. Sometimes I speak aloud, sometimes in my head, depending on the amount of people. And yesterday, no one was on the path, so I asked him out loud, "Can you believe the life we are living in?" I released one of those small, bitter laughs and said, "Well, *I'm* living in. You're dead." Then I proceeded to spout off to Peter all I held inside, like I always did.

While walking the final few minutes of the path, a hawk flew overhead. A hawk always appears in the sky when I'm out there. Maybe it's a natural occurrence. Maybe hawks like wetlands. But I think it's Peter letting me know he is with me. I'll be honest, when I saw the hawk, I was momentarily jealous of the freedom of its flight, since it reminded me how Peter has been released of all life's worries. He doesn't live the life I do because he died first, even though that wasn't our deal. I asked him to be with me, help me be the fighter we both know I am, help me figure out the path I now have to walk, without him, and to ask God, the Universe, all the people who went before me and now are my angels, to show me my purpose in all of this. And when I got home, I cried.

I miss Peter all the time. I miss him during this time of COVID. I miss talking to Peter and holding him. I miss how he somehow made me feel in our more intimate moments. All of that is gone now because all of him is gone now, which only makes me feel more helpless.

I was empty last night, truly empty. It wasn't just grief's fault. It was life's too, for all the messed-up things it's holding right now.

Releasing More of Him

Within an hour, Peter's stuff will be leaving. My family has all kept some of his stuff, but the other stuff, the whatchamacallits, the thingamajigs, and the whatsits will all be gone. All of the doodads, the broken-down furniture, the equipment that needs to be fixed, the materials for a project never fulfilled, will be gone today, and my heart is heavy.

I was excited at first, and part of me still is. Purging things that I will never use and only take up space—so much space—is necessary to me. To live among the long strips of wood that were once crown molding in my living room, or the PVC pipes saved for possible use in the garden, or the broken futon Peter was one day going to fix, is claustrophobic to me. It is stuff that clutters a space in a house I am may or may not sell.

I hired a company who will go through the stuff to either salvage, donate, or recycle the clutter in my house, which eases my mind. And yet, as the stuff leaves, as his stuff leaves, I will see parts of Peter leave me for a final time, and my heart will break a little. I know I'll cry. I always cry. I'm not second-guessing my decision. I think once it's all gone and I let go of all my emotions—in an hour, a day, a week, a month, however long it takes—it'll be okay, perhaps even freeing. I have no emotional attachment to any of the things leaving today. Not like the attachment I have to my wedding ring, or photographs, or his love letters to me. I don't hold the same emotion to a piece of plywood or deflated basketballs than I do to the souvenir turtle he bought on one of our vacations. Still, the stuff serves as reminders of who Peter was, why he was so special. They tell stories of his creativity, his brilliance, his desire to always have a project. Releasing all of it is going to be painful.

What I am finding out this morning is that the memories of *Peter's* attachment to these things have set me back to a hard grief. But I know I have to let them go. They are Peter's things with no purpose for me. Holding onto things because of what they meant to Peter will crowd me, and I can't move when I'm jammed in place. After all the stuff is gone, I'll be able to sit and think, in a house emptied out. In this empty and new canvas, I can start painting my own life, without him. I know Peter would want me to let go. It was his stuff, his ideas, and along with him, they are dead. I can't hold onto them and still move toward what's to come.

Some have suggested it's too soon to let go of all his things. Others said they would have walked away a lot sooner. I only know myself. And even though it won't be easy for me this morning—letting go never is—I know deep inside, it is my time to release more of him.

I Sobbed Yesterday

I sobbed yesterday. I sobbed because the house is emptied out, and I felt empty. I sobbed because I don't know how to live in this place we once called home. I sobbed because the house doesn't feel like anything now but a building I sit in. I sobbed yesterday because if I do stay, it will be mine and not ours. I sobbed because, even slowly, I do have to get there, and I don't know where the hell "there" is. And I sobbed yesterday because this, all of this, falls on me alone, and no one understands it because I am the one living without Peter.

I sobbed yesterday because of the infinite number of choices that lie ahead of me, and I don't know how to grab them. I sobbed because I am so tired of people telling me, "You'll know when it's right," and "Take your time," and "It's all so new," and "One day at time/baby steps." I sobbed because sometimes I can't hold back my frustration and I want to shout at people, "Taking time and waiting is painful, so stop preaching tolerance to me!" I sobbed because allowing the Universe/God to somehow open up to show me the right time and to give me those comforting moments never settles me. I sobbed because normalcy is what I long for, yet I still feel I am on this constant ride to nowhere. I sobbed because I just want people to fucking listen to me without telling me how I should act or what will eventually happen, especially those who don't know this journey. And I sobbed because I don't want to be made to feel bad or wrong somehow for wanting an end point.

I sobbed yesterday because I am alone in all of this. I sobbed because I wake up, spend my day, and say goodnight to myself, by myself. I sobbed because the emptiness of an apartment, of a house, surrounds me every day. I sobbed because I once had someone who was in my space but is suddenly forever gone, and I never wanted it or chose it or got any closure. I sobbed because it's almost so many fucking months later, and I ache like I did when he first died; only now I am better at living with it. I sobbed because I am better at living with it. And I sobbed yesterday because even with the smile I strangle out of me, even with the perception of strength, even with the moving on, I am still hurting and people forget that.

I sobbed yesterday because my dog, Barkley, sat on my lap while I cried, until a fly caught his interest and he jumped off. I sobbed because, like my dog, people's lives are distracted by things flying by them, while I sit and sob about my own reality. I sobbed because that is the way of the world, the way it happens, and it's unfair. I sobbed because there were people who never cared, still don't care, and won't ever care. I sobbed because there were people who never told me they cared or were cruel to me with their words during my weakest moments. And I sobbed yesterday because so many people do care and will always care, and I love them all for it.

I sobbed yesterday because the pent-up anger, frustration, sadness, agony, and loneliness I carry around with me every day choke me. I sobbed because I carry around all these emotions I can't put into words. I sobbed because Peter was the now and then, in my here and now, for me. I sobbed because I am a widow, and with that is the inability to ever be Peter's wife, here on Earth. And I sobbed yesterday because feeling and hearing are two different things and I don't know, really know, will never know, if Peter hears me, and I sobbed, especially, because I don't hear him.

I sobbed yesterday because I was in the swells of self-pity. I sobbed because I loathe the self-centered person I've become, the self-centered person I never wanted to be. I sobbed because grief has robbed me of who I once was and being alone makes it hard to see who I am now, who I will become. I sobbed because of all the good people in my life and the blessings in all of them. And I sobbed yesterday, because in spite of them, even with them, I feel defeated.

This morning, as the sun lightens a new day with new possibilities, I know I have a day of cleaning ahead of me. I have a day of moving boxes in their rightful spots and organizing. I have a day of walks with Barkley and writing words. And I have a day full of thoughts and feelings with a hope that on this day the sobs will be less or even gone, and I can push through it all. But yesterday I sobbed because it was a bad day and I needed to.

Pages in a Murky Field

I want to improve. I want to be this badass who faces the world with my hands on my hips, my head thrown back, and lets out a laugh at the challenges in front of me. I want to take on the world with the energy of an overactive toddler. I want to get things accomplished. I want to be happy to fuel my energy. I want to make decisions and stick with them. I want to make plans and go through with them. I want all of this, to be all of this. I really do. And yet I can't. Not now.

I grew up with a park across the street from me. The park had swing sets, monkey bars, and those always dangerous teeter-totters. It also had three baseball fields. I would spend my days running back and forth through the fields to play on all the park's equipment, then run back through them again to go home. I didn't stick to the sidewalks leading to the park. Running and open land was who I was.

One afternoon, after a night of heavy storms, after I took the sidewalks to get to the playground, I chose the muddy, murky dirt of the flooded baseball fields to come home. It was getting late and I knew I had to be home for supper. Not far in, I reached a point where I couldn't move. The mud cemented me in place and paralyzed me behind second base of the largest of the ball fields.

My brother and his friend, my next-door neighbor, were across the street and I screamed for help. They came and stood on the sidewalk figuring out how to get me to move. Eventually, my neighbor tore the pages out of his comic book and used them as steps toward me. Then, he picked me up, and using those same pages as footfalls, he carried me to the sidewalk.

I thought about this story this morning because I feel as stuck as I did when I was planted in the mud all those years ago. I am looking for the comic book pages so I can move and get to some sort of safety. It seems every time I step on the one in front of me, I hesitate, or pull back in uncertainty. And I can only see one page, not an entire path laid before me. The man who carried me through life is now dead, and I've been dropped in a flooded field of confusion. Peter was the logic, the patience, and the calm to my impulsiveness, my restlessness, and my angst. I have to retrain my active mind, piece together my jumbled thoughts, slow down my jump-ahead conclusions, and focus. It's all up to me and I don't know where to go with it.

I have made some decisions, though. Getting my dog, Barkley, was huge and a decision which proved to be exactly what I needed. I have slowed in deciding where to live or when to move. I am not in a hurry. Pulling back on the purchase of two homes because of uncertainty, not feeling like it was right for right now, showed me I don't have to rush to any conclusions. And the decision I made to remove Peter's stuff from this house—stuff with no history or value, but stuff his engineering brain thought of ways to create with (and so many times he did)—was a great one, despite the pain of letting go. Yet, I still feel lost without Peter, and still question my capabilities.

I suppose I should look back at the pages I have already walked on instead of the emptiness in front of me and grow some confidence, some pride, and be encouraged. I have to have faith in the Universe, in God, and most especially in myself, that future pages will come before me soon enough. I need to realize the path ahead of me may not be the one Peter would have walked on, or even would have agreed with, but it will be my path and mine alone. Peter is never coming back, and I am still here.

As hard as it is this morning, I have to convince myself to find the energy within me to take more steps in the murky field of grief, of longing, of being on my own after thirty-two years of being with Peter. I have to wait for the pages to come, and they will come in an eventuality I need to be patient with. Until then, perhaps I should take the time to stand still and take in the peace of what I have now, the pages I have stepped on thus far, and stop trying to hurry through the muddiness of emotions, consequences, despair, and grief.

I want to have the ability to conquer it all, conquer it now, to walk on top of the murk because I am so tired of standing still in it. I hear distant whispers warning me not to move just yet and instead think of the direction I want to go. Those whispers just may be from the badass emerging inside of me, the one who will plant my life's pages in front of her and move one step at time.

Sitting Under the Maple Tree with Nobody Else but Me . . . and Barkley

I sit out in my backyard most warm nights and take in the beauty of my yard. Barkley comes out with me and sits in the dirt under a plant he uses for shade. It's a beautiful yard, a peaceful one. It's a yard filled with Peter memories since the yard is Peter. Peter worked hard in making it an oasis, perhaps for our older years together, most likely to leave his footprint for the years ahead, for others to enjoy after us.

Peter was a gardener. He planted flowers, wild grass, and trees for their beauty, to attract birds and butterflies, and for privacy. He showed his love for me by honing his gardening skills. When I would say in passing, "Hydrangeas are so beautiful," or "I had a Rose of Sharon in my front yard growing up," he planted both for me. He knew I loved the one lilac bush in our yard, so he planted three more. When he was done, pride always beamed off of him, looking like the young man I dated who was eager to impress.

Every Mother's Day, Peter would take me out to buy flowers for the front. I didn't have much to say about the types. Peter did his research, and I rode his coattail. I had confidence that he knew which ones would grow best. He would ask me the colors I wanted. I would tell him, and he would either agree or ask, "How about these?" and pick out another color. I didn't mind. The joy I saw on his face while we walked through the garden store was gift enough for me. Besides, my attachment to flowers was not nearly as strong as his.

Peter also adored his vegetable garden. It was something he grew up with and loved to do. I think it gave him a connection back to his roots. Yes, I get the pun. Peter built a three-tier vegetable garden. The tiers allowed for better water distribution. Every spring, around the second weekend in March, he made a mini greenhouse around the garden for the seeds' protection. From then on, Peter meticulously weeded and watered tomatoes, cilantro, pumpkins, various lettuce, Brussels sprouts, potatoes, rhubarb, and peppers in all sorts of colors. What we couldn't eat, we shared with neighbors or the local food banks.

This week, as I sat in my backyard under the huge maple tree a young boy planted before we purchased the house over twenty-five years ago, I talked to Peter. *I bought some flowers for the front this week*, I told him. *Don't ask me what kind. They were pretty and the instructions said they were hardy. Good enough for me.* Then I laughed, knowing he would smile his crooked smile, maybe chuckle, maybe shake his head, probably all three. *I didn't get a lot. I mean, it looks fine, but I am sure it's not your version of fine. But you're not here anymore, so I suppose I have to go with my fine.*

The conversation dug some loneliness out of me. I thought Peter and I should be sitting out there, together, holding hands, he with a beer, and me with a glass of wine. It's not like we ever did this, though. When he was alive, I was more a ten-minutes-and-I'm-inside person. Mosquitoes love my allergic self. They never bothered Peter. But for some reason, I conjured up this picture of us, in our old age, or older age. Hopes for future things together, he and I, died with him and add to the agony of my soul. It doesn't stop my mind from drifting there as I find myself out in the backyard more often, almost every night, mosquitoes be damned. I'm not sure why I sit there, other than trying to connect with Peter, to the memories of once-was and trying to find answers to what will become.

Last night was a very lonely night for me. The heaviness of missing Peter weighed on me like the humidity of the daytime. Weekend nights are unpredictable to me still. I miss him the most on Friday and Saturday nights. These nights, even with young kids, were our time. Now it's Barkley-and-me time. So, as Barkley and I sat in the yard, I just let myself be me. I talked to Peter a little, dwelled on my emptiness of him, and I let the tears come, not bothering to block it or push it away. And I felt him.

I felt him in the hummingbird dancing by the Rose of Sharon and in the color exploding from a flower I can't name and growing out of the rhubarb still left behind. I felt it in a way that was new to me. It wasn't just in a longing for him, or self-pity. I also felt a sadness in looking at all he did for me and wishing I could have appreciated it all the more when he was alive. I used to think this wouldn't happen to me, the death of Peter. I put off or ignored words to say and emotions to share until a tomorrow. Then those tomorrows never came for me.

After Peter died, most of his inside plants and all of his vegetable garden died with him. Maybe they held too much of a reminder for me to tend to them. Maybe my inability to even move, let alone take care of anything, destroyed them. Maybe they weren't mine to cultivate. Or maybe all of the above. Regardless, they all died. The vegetable garden is left intact without any plants in it, but the three tiers full of dirt are ready for the next owner(s) to create what they will with them. When I move, the flowers and bushes and trees will stay with the house, the way I feel Peter intended for them. Nature is not ours alone to keep, but for us to nurture for the next.

I will be moving soon. This house has grown too big for Barkley and me. I am rebuilding something smaller in the same town, the town of my heart. This is my last summer in Peter's yard. I know I will have new bushes and flowers and trees in my new place. New memories, memories without Peter, will spring from them. Still, it will be hard to walk away. And yet, whether I sit this summer in the yard Peter created, or next summer in my new one, every time I get a whiff of lilacs or see a bud on a Rose of Sharon, I will make it a point to say, *Thank you, Peter. I was a lucky woman.*

The Day After . . .

Yesterday, the first-year mark of Peter's death, I pretended the outside world didn't exist. My phone pinged with texts, phone calls, and messages via Facebook. Most knew I wasn't responding. Not all wanted or expected a response. They were sending a simple, *"I'm thinking of you today."* Flowers were delivered and put on my doorstep. Friends offered meals. And there were pictures of Peter on social media commemorating the first-year mark. Even though the outside world disappeared from me, friends made sure I didn't disappear from it.

I took a long nap a few hours after I woke up in the morning, hoping I would (as Peter used to call napping) time travel through the day. When I was awake, I sat and stared, stared and sat, not really having words to share with my kids, nor them with me. What can we say anyway? The unspoken words hung over us in a heavy cloud of sorrow, and it didn't need to rain on us. We knew. It was nice having my kids around. There is bonding in shared pain.

Of course, I thought about Peter. I think about him all the time, and yesterday was no exception. I thought how much I have lost since he died. I even replayed the day of his death in my mind with a sick game of *"one year ago today at this time . . ."* I'm not sure why I did. It didn't help nor did it hinder. It just was. And during this playing out of the day a year ago game, it hit me, as it does every time, how I had him, and then he was gone.

The day ended with a shared meal with my kids, mindless TV, and in the loneliness of my bedroom, shedding some tears as I reflected back on the year and thought about the second year ahead. Some experienced members of this widow club no one wants to be in told me the second year won't be as hard. Other members said it will be harder. Still others sighed, saying it will be just more of the same. I guess it depends on the widow. I wonder though, going into my second year, if people will expect it's now my time to let go of my grief and move on with my life. I wonder if people will listen to my woes and think, *Enough already.* I wonder if people will listen at all. I carry with me insecurities of people's perceptions. I shouldn't, but I do. I am getting closer to not caring. I have a long way to go in my travels to get there, but I am heading that way. Until then, last night, the thoughts circled my head instead of sheep. I know grief grows tiresome, especially for the one grieving.

When I woke this morning, I thought only one thought about the upcoming second year for me . . . *I don't know.* I don't know if a second year without Peter will change much inside of me. He will still be dead. I will still miss him, as much as I missed him the day he died. Years can't take that from me. Perhaps, though, I will learn to live with the pain like a marathon runner in the second lap of the course. I will learn to live with the blisters and the side stitches as I continue on. I want to look forward, to the experiences ahead of me, even if they are in the shadows of once-was. After dealing with Peter's death for a year now, I know more pain, anger, longing, and all the different emotions grief hands to me, will not make Peter a part of my living life anymore. It doesn't mean I will suddenly stop feeling any of these emotions. What it does mean though, is that I can move with them. I think I am stronger now and will continue to get stronger, at least enough to move with them on my back and not be as weighed down. In the end though, I just don't know . . .

I don't know why I was ever handed this in my life, not this early, not this abruptly, and without final goodbyes and *I love you's*. I don't understand, and going into the second year, I still don't. I won't ever understand. And that's where so much of my pain comes from, this repetitive question of *why me?* I will *never, ever* be able to come near grasping the big "Fuck You" that life gave me when it let Peter move on with death.

Coming into this second year, I know I am a different person. I am starting to regrow the part of me that was ripped out when he died. I am starting to stand up and face the challenges ahead of me. And I want to get to the part of life where I feel the good as equally as the bad. Lately, I have felt numb, and I will take it, as it's better than feeling the sadness that filled me for most of the last year. At the same time, I have had more glimpses of being happy now, which is a good thing, a great thing, a needed thing. Because here it is and here I am, a widow going into her second year, moving on this unwanted path death paved for me.

PART IV

Follow Me Forward

Restlessness

There is a restlessness growing inside me. It encourages me to keep on, even when my spirit is in question. It warns me to avoid too frequent glances backward, lest I trip on what's ahead of me. It reminds me of my reality often with a shrug of, "Okay, so now what?" It gets aggressive when I slip into what-if's, once-were's, and I-wish's.

This restlessness started to peak out at the beginning of COVID. I think boredom and claustrophobia may have pushed it out for an appearance. During the solitude of COVID, I started to see who I can be without Peter. Being alone with myself, inside my memories and thoughts, stirred a restless desire for change and difference. Restlessness creeps into my nighttime as I lie in bed. The crickets' serenade makes me focus on my possibilities. I see the new path I need to take in my mind's eyes, the one to travel on without concern or fret about people's opinions. This restlessness makes me want to snap at people in a this-is-who-I-am-now impatience in the daylight hours. I have agitation growing from my want for others to see me now, not who I once was. Unfair of me, I know. The once-was is what they see in me. I am only now introducing them to who is evolving.

The other night, I sat around a neighbor's fire pit. A few of the neighbors talked and shared about their lives amid this pandemic. It was a lovely night to be out with a common thread among us. I told a story of having time now to rip out old insulation from my basement. I spoke about the abandoned vermin nests, dried up wasps' nests, and insect eggs that came down with the insulation. It was a gross undertaking, but one expected in a basement of a certain age, especially from a house near wetlands. One of my neighbors was in slight disbelief that it was me, really me, who tore it all down and swept it all out. I don't blame her. I held that same disbelief when I completed the project.

Like so many other people in my life who only knew me with Peter, she still sees me as this Peter-reliant person, the person I have been for these past twenty-eight years. My restlessness does not let me stay that person, with reminders of, "You can't anymore because he's not here anymore." Besides, I couldn't if I wanted to, because the Peter part of me is gone now. This friend also expressed pride in me for getting it done. When she did, my restlessness became arrogant with a whisper of, "See."

When Peter first died, I didn't want to change. I wanted to be the same. I blocked out any thoughts of entertaining any change. My life was so out of control, and I wanted, no needed, to remain the same. I avoided anything that may test my boundaries or demonstrate my need to change. I kept my house as-is for a while. I allowed my kids to take over some of the finances. I existed in a fog and, since I couldn't see ahead of me, I didn't try. It wasn't a bad thing. It was a survival thing. Oh, I rented an apartment, but only to escape what I didn't want to face—the memories of him and the us-centered house. Then restlessness came and forced me to look at the inevitable need to emerge from the ashes because Peter was gone now. I wouldn't say I liked it at first. But I knew I would have to give in.

My restlessness has challenged me to take down insulation and all the icky stuff with it. It shoves me onto a path of creating my own living space. It put a fire in me to allow this new person to emerge while deafening me to criticism along the way. It gives me permission to make mistakes, learn from them, and grow from them. It shows me over and over that I am not the same person anymore.

When I started in widowhood, I mourned Peter and all he meant. I grieved not only him but my reliance upon him. Now, my restlessness invades me and asks me, "*Okay, now what?*" There is new grief in this. Walking alone can be painful without Peter. Yet, I know these are the steps I need to take now, even if I walk gingerly with anxious hesitation. I am both scared and excited to walk my new path and look at what I have accomplished along the way. I have so much more ahead of me and will tackle each step because I am now restless.

Starting Over

I have to start over. At an age most people are settled in comfortably with their lives and secure in who they are, I have no choice but to begin again. Yes, I have a foundation to build on. It is a strong one having stood the test of time and experiences. Since Peter died, now I have no choice but to wreck parts of the sandcastle I built with Peter in order to erect a new one. I'll be honest, I don't know how because I am still learning who I am without him.

When I rented an apartment downtown, I thought it might give me some answers. Getting away from the memories and the reminders of Peter, even the people who only knew me with him, seemed healing to me. The thought of going back to the city of my birth, the city I love, gave me a settling familiarity. The city served as a reminder of a place in time where I was care-free and felt cocooned in love and infallibility that youth often tricks us with. The possibilities of places to go, people to see, and culture to suck up like a thirsty patron of this world, seem to hold some answers to the quest of finding myself without Peter. Only, it didn't work out that way . . . not the way I thought anyway.

Oh, I needed my apartment. I know I needed it. After Peter died, I needed to get away from the house's memories to sort out all of my thoughts and feelings, without any connection to Peter. I wanted to be in the midst of the noise and crowds and chaos that had nothing to do with Peter's death, but everything to do with memories of my past. It was like running into the arms of an old lover to find distraction and comfort only familiarity brings. And it worked . . . for a while . . . until it didn't. While the city lays out in front of me all of its possibilities, two things keep me from grasping them—loneliness and my still emerging self.

When you are given solitude without permission, without want, it can be paralyzing, at least for me. Seeing a play, going to a museum, meeting people, even taking a walk along the riverfront, only feeds into my lonesomeness, only feeds into my deep loss of him. They don't offer distractions, rather reminders. Perhaps if Peter were alive, and I could count on him to be my touchstone, like he always was for me, things would be different. But he isn't alive. He'll never be alive again. And that is the cruel, hard fact I face anytime I try something, alone, without him.

When I meet new people since Peter died, the outcomes have not been the best. Most of the time, not knowing who I am yet erects barricades. I found talking to new people easy once, but now it's hard. All of my resolve depletes, and I just want ease. I want people to know me where I am at and not take them to the beginning. Thus, the results are awkward attempts which fuel my insecurities.

Funny thing is though, when I lived in my apartment, I left behind the people who did know me. I left behind a community who reached out to me when I had the flu asking what I needed. I left behind a community who made cookies for my book signing. I left behind a community where I have people to have lunch with, go to Trivia with, see a movie with and just be myself around, even if I don't quite have a grip on who that is right now. I left behind a community who knows the underlying me and is more than willing to embrace what emerges. While in my apartment, I find myself wanting to be with the people who knew me with Peter because part of me is because of Peter. Sometimes, when you run away, you run in circles.

So where do I go from here? I honestly don't know. I know my apartment's purpose is different from what I sought in the beginning, yet it does have a purpose. It has given me, and continues to give me, a productive place to write and think and still look at all the possibilities. It has shown me where I am meant to be and not where I romanticize myself to be. I still have this from-the-belly joy of the city I can't describe. I'm doing something I haven't done, or have done little of, since being on this reluctant journey. I'm being patient, taking time to think it through. Perhaps my apartment has given me patience as well.

As I delve deeper into who I am, I have begun to rule out who I am not. It's part of starting over. I have to admit, beginning to live again has been my hardest challenge . . . ever. One I might not have asked for, but here I am, at my age, facing it. So, let's go, Life. Bring it on.

Letter To Peter

Dear Peter,

I have been thinking about what I miss in you, in us, in our marriage. The simple things come to mind, along with the deep things and the routine things. I miss all of them, all of you.

I miss your smile. I miss the way light reached your eyes and wrinkles crinkled around them. The way it could be crooked sometimes and thinned out the next. The way it softened your ruddy face and made others around you smile with you, to you. The way it was given with understanding, or joy, or in a tease. The way it lit up in joy from the loves you held in your life, especially nature, your children, and me. The way your smile made me feel as though we had happiness in our world, a part which I gave you.

I miss your body, how it was in constant motion doing the things in life you loved. How it moved in a shuffle, with your lanky legs in lengthy, slow strides, pushing aside the earth in front of you. How your body was all long-limbed, even long fingers and toes. How every part of you was thin, yet strong and muscle-packed. The body which would lie next to me and hold me and make me feel secure in its presence.

I miss your mind. The one filled with so many beautiful thoughts. The one which figured out the most complex of problems as if they were nursey rhymes. The one which thirsted for knowledge from books, videos, explorations, and absorbed everything like a sponge, never wanting wringing. The one which shared its contents with your children, with me, with the world. The mind which awed and inspired friends, family, coworkers, and me. The mind which grounded my own unsettled one.

I miss your love of life. The feeling of intrigue from anything as tiny as an ant, to as large as an elephant, and everything in between. The feeling of freedom you got from gliding a boat over choppy waters or riding a motorcycle through the gusts of winds. The feeling of joy from a new powdered snow you could cross-country ski on, or the discovery of new trails to hike on. The feeling of accomplishment from digging your hands in dirt to produce a food or pulling the weeds away from the flowers you cultivated. The love of life you felt every time nature called to you, leaving me to revel in your stories.

I miss your parenting. The need of giving our children your attention from their infancy to adulthood. The need to advise and the knowledge to pull back. The need to unconditionally love them, accepting them for who they were, and eventually meeting at the place they were at. The need to have fun with them, at any age, enjoying the moments as they unfolded. The need of teaching them, expanding their minds, showing them experiences with a patience envied by most. The need to acknowledge their continual necessity for you into adulthood. Your parenting aided me and taught me and partnered with me to have these most amazing, unique, kind adults now. Mostly, I miss us, the repetition of us. The routine of waking up with, "Good morning." The routine laid out with going to work, coming home, eating dinner, and going to bed. The routine of texts when something exciting happens, or mundane information of what to pick up for dinner. The routine of chores, TV shows, looking for appliances, visiting friends and families, and of being alone, together. The routine of saying and hearing, "I love you." The routine of taking for granted moments, the security of one love, the knowledge of growing old together. The routines aren't always the moments you remember the most, but they are the ones missed the most.

There are days when my heart fills with all that I miss, all I want back, all I know will never be again. These are the days I smile the most and remember the vows we took in front of God, friends, and family all those years ago, which were never broken, because we never broke, that is until your death shattered me.

I have picked up so many of the pieces, month by month. Less lie on the ground now than when you died. Yet still some fragments remain scattered around me. Today, flooding memories of us make it too difficult for me to pick those up right now. They are reminders of what I miss reflected back at me, and I have no strength to even stoop down. Not today. Today, I will ignore them, walk around them, without the worries of when I will gather them in again. Make no mistake, I will gather them again because I need to, because I have to, because I want to. But for today, I will think about the things I miss about you, us, our marriage and hold them in the place of my heart where grief took up residency on the day you were killed.

Accidental Repercussions

It was five o'clock on a Monday. I was roused from a late afternoon doze in a chair by a persistent knock on my front door. I went to the door and peered out its side window. A strapping police officer appearing larger by the bulletproof vest he wore stood on my stoop. My heart raced at the sight of an officer of the law at my home. I flashed back to every television cop show I have watched over the years and concluded a murder occurred in my sleepy neighborhood. I opened the door in hesitation and anxious anticipation.

After the police officer identified himself, he asked if I was Mrs. Dudak. When I responded with a nod, he followed up with the question if Peter was my husband. Again, I nodded. He pushed a piece of paper at me and told me to call that number. He explained that my husband was in the hospital because of an accident, and I needed to call right away. Instinctively, I shook his hand and thanked him. Looking back, I laugh a little over the thought of thanking him for telling me the bad news.

When I arrived at the hospital, the doctor said the words that forever changed my life, "We did all we could." She explained how a man driving a Ram pickup truck went through an intersection and smashed into Peter on his motorcycle, killing him instantly. The memories from the events that followed—collapsing onto Peter's lifeless, cold body, the blood under Peter's fingernails, seeing his broken nose and all the tubes coming out of him, and spending the last moments as a family in a morgue—still give me trauma.

In months to come, I would know more about what happened. The man driving the truck was seventy-eight. When he came up to an intersection of a four-lane highway, either he stopped and then took off to beat oncoming traffic, or he ignored the stop sign altogether. On this, I am uncertain. Either way, the result was that his vehicle struck Peter while on his motorcycle, killing him. The driver received a failure to yield ticket, the same ticket given to someone who blew a stop sign without the result of death. Illinois does not differentiate, even if the failure to yield results in death.

The collision caused Peter to fly off his bike and onto his head, breaking his neck. The paramedics on the scene and the doctor at the hospital felt Peter died from the moment of impact. The doctor said, if she were wrong about her death on impact theory, Peter would have died shortly after that from a broken neck. Whichever way he died, he did not suffer. At the time, this did not offer me any comfort, as I only reeled from the finality of Peter's death. But, as more months went by, I was extremely relieved my husband did not suffer. Besides the fact that he would have been a miserable patient, I am glad he left this world instantaneously and without pain.

In the days and months that followed the accident, I didn't spend too much time thinking about the driver. The times I did were when many people said to me something to the effect of, "Imagine the hell he's living in." To which I snapped back with, "Probably not as hot as the hell my kids and I are in now."

I'm not sure why people say things without thinking when someone dies. Maybe grief overwhelms them, and stupidity results. They can't believe those words would be a comfort. Seriously, why would someone tell a person whose entire world has just been upended and is struggling to hold it together for her children, to think about the driver? What kind of solace does that bring? Should I have responded by saying, "You're right, and now I'm done grieving"? I didn't get it then, and I still don't understand it now. Sometimes, the best thing to do is remain silent.

There were things I chose not to do in response to the accident. I never wanted to destroy the man who hit him or his family. When I first met with the state's attorney before I knew what Illinois law allowed, I told everyone in the room I did not want the man in jail for this. Before settling, I said to my civil lawyer that I didn't want to take everything from him, only what his insurance allowed. I am not now, nor was I then, a martyr. I am and was a woman with a focus on survival and the well-being of my children. I did not want to make money off my husband's death, nor would the destruction of a man's life make my life any better. Besides, nothing I felt, didn't feel, did, or didn't do, would bring back Peter. He died—the how part is moot.

The man's sentencing trial took a year and a half. The delay had nothing to do with guilt or innocence.

Witnesses and a police reenactment proved straight-out responsibility. The wait was because of COVID. When the sentencing trial took place, it did so on Peter's sixtieth birthday, an odd and painful coincidence. I recounted to the court and the man the pain and longing I have lived in since Peter died in my victim's statement. I also introduced them to Peter by educating them on his background and life before his death. I didn't want Peter's memory lost in the formality of the hearing. I ended my statement by asking the court to consider suspending the man's license and community service. I wanted some consequences for the death of Peter, if only to recognize his importance in this world.

The driver's lawyer informed the court of the driver's impeccable driving record, his service to his community, and the remorse this man felt since the accident. When it was the driver's turn to speak, he did so with a shaky voice. He told the court and me that he thinks about Peter every day since the accident. It is something he wakes up with and goes to bed thinking. He swore, he never saw Peter coming, and he wished he could do it all over again. He apologized to my family and me for taking Peter's life.

His words caused sobs to come out from a deep part of me. His words lifted some weight off my chest as if he said what I felt all along, none of it was ever intentional, yet I needed to hear those words. I had no reason to doubt his sincerity, or his need for forgiveness then or now. Without being able to speak anymore in the courtroom, I sent up to the universe a silent acceptance to the man's apology. I hope he received it. We both needed it.

In the end, the man, now over eighty, received a sentence of payment for court fees and a year of court probation in which he could not commit any crime. Due to COVID, his wife's health, and his health, the man did not receive community service, nor was his license suspended. Afterward, I couldn't speak to the fairness or unfairness of this sentence. I just knew it was, and now I had to move on.

The other day, I was talking to my daughter about my relief of closing the door on the court case and, subsequently, the accident part of Peter's death story. Having the sentencing linger for months served as a blockade toward my goal now of living without Peter. Closing it seemed to clear the path of my life up ahead. I told her I never felt like the accident was significant enough to keep open this long. The accident described how Peter died but did not have a part of what was missing because of his death. My thoughts, feelings, and concentration have always been on the finality of Peter's death, not on the accident, and maybe that's why I don't hold anger or hatred toward the driver. My daughter nodded and then summed everything I felt brilliantly. She said, "It's never been about the moment. It's always been about the repercussions of that moment." What she said.

Change of Status

As I move on in my life without Peter, I've started to make my own purchases like a new home, new insurance, new mortgage, and new credit cards. Boxes require me to check, single, married, and sometimes, widow on the application forms. When I check the single or the widow box, I feel an emptiness and an uncomfortable shock.

I was widowed young. Maybe not as young as some, but too young to have the words my husband died apply to me and my description. I didn't think they would pertain to me until well into my eighties. But they do and when I say my husband died, or even describe Peter as my late husband, the words stammer out of me in unfamiliarity. The words are not easy to say, and I'm not sure they will ever be easy. Perhaps they will become more manageable, but I don't think I'll ever be at total ease admitting my husband is no longer part of my living life.

In my close circle of friends, where spouses are still alive, my status change makes me feel like a bit of a novelty. I try to fit in as I once did. When my friends tell tales about their husbands or wives, I reflexively jump in with a Peter-story of my own. Though, unlike their stories, mine is of the past, not the present. I know, as time passes, my contribution to spousal anecdotes will be further in my past. One day, they will become nostalgic tales told like childhood memories or wild stories of my twenties. It's not that I don't want to share my stories of Peter. He will always be part of my life. Yet starting my stories as *once upon a time* is odd and uncomfortable to me, even painful at times.

There is also a certain disconnect when I try to throw in a story of Peter with my friends when they tell their own spousal stories. It feels as if a line has broken, which was part of the multi-line connection between my friends and me. I am sure, in time, I will become more comfortable with the severed lines. I already see new ones forming.

Some friends have become closer to me, and us to each other, since Peter died. Besides their compassion to me in all of this, a newness has grown between us. Something different has formed other than our "men" eye rolls or our, "That happened to me too," common ground. Perhaps because our friendship no longer hinges on our partners, we have gravitated toward sharing more and different things about ourselves, our solo selves. I also have formed evolving friendships of former acquaintances who I may have never known at this other level, this single level. I can think of three women I did not know well, but we are now differently bonded because of our shared widowhood.

On the other hand, I have let go of other relationships after Peter's death. They were never present for me when Peter died. They continued to avoid me in the months after his death, without explanation or apology. A few even became defensive when I questioned their absence. I have come to realize these were the weaker relationships in my life. Sometimes, the weakest ones are those formed by circumstances. Once the circumstance changes or breaks, so does the relationship. I have begun to look at my widowhood as a vetting out of people in my life, people I hung onto longer than I should have.

I imagine my widowhood status, my single one, is a lot like divorce or like those who have always been single. I can't speak fully on either, yet they must hold some of the same emotions. While I never want to compare my apples to their oranges, they're both fruits of our new existence. In the end, we are all single. While our reasons are different, the status remains the same—single.

Widowhood has a strong association with so much. It is a word to describe being single after being part of a whole. It has been hard to put down single or widow status on a form or talk about it now as my reality. I grapple with my new status daily, even trying to trick myself into believing I'm not one. Facts always bring me back. I don't have to mark a box on a form to convince myself. And so, I continue embracing the change in my status, and with it, all the possibilities it can hold. I will give nods to the past, but I will continue to walk toward my future without Peter, as a single, widowed woman. I am alive, so I must live.

New Year, New Beginning

It's a new year and one and half years without Peter in my life. I am starting to change more. I moved past so much of what held me back in the beginning. The emotions I had initially, the strong, intense ones, are starting to diminish, and I find myself living more and surviving less. This living has been my most significant sign of growing with the grief. I don't think I'll ever go past grief. It'll always be my constant companion. I do feel, though, its importance has lessened in my Life.

My Life has started to take me in other directions. I am taking an honest and real look at living as a widow, and all that means—navigation without a partner, suddenly single as I near sixty, wondering who I am to become, and most importantly, accepting who I am already. This candid assessment of my Life scared me in the beginning. It was an admission I would live the rest of my Life without Peter in it. I avoided that thought like I would a horror movie. Now though, it scares me less. Instead of an anxious rumination, it has become a surprise thought or a sad backstory.

I have started to see glimpses into myself I never saw in my marriage when I had a partner to lean on. I have gained the strength to stand on my own because Life's all on me now. I don't have anyone to consider when making decisions. The new house I am having built and its decor will reflect me, and me alone. Any mistakes I make are mine with no one to blame or share the blame. The same goes for my successes. I may even celebrate those more now as I know I alone own them. Every definition of me is about only me. Sure, it can be scary at times, yet with so much excitement thrown in.

There is a strange emergence of myself different from when Peter was alive. I had relied on Peter for so much. At times, I depended on his approval, accepted his opinion over mine, and conceded to his choices. Parts of my decisions were marriage's natural compromises. Other parts were my insecurities, abandonment issues, and trying my best to please Peter, for he meant everything to me. Now with him gone, I have to be my own person, and there have been growths and changes foreign to me because of this. I acknowledge that mistakes will continue, and I don't try to fight the inevitability of them. Peter's death by no means wipes away any of my problems. But I am forced to deal with them more, head-on, and without hiding behind Peter. I have started to do just that, and in the process, I don't beat myself up nearly as much with worry and instead tell myself *it'll be okay because* everything pales in comparison to Peter's death.

To my surprise, I have fewer battles with patience since Peter died, which is so different from the married me. I had always lost my patience when I lost control. Peter's death has taught me there are so many things in life out of my control. I have also learned what I do have control over is all on me.

I am working on accepting what happened and what my life is now because of it. It is not lost on me that the final stage of grief is acceptance. I also know just because I'm in this stage does not mean I won't be hopping backward to other stages I don't visit as often. I don't think as frequently, though, because I feel different lately.

Peter's death was horrible, and the suddenness of it was horrific. I miss him every day. I never asked for any of this. I never wanted any of this. I never dreamed any of this. I still shed tears from my longing for him. I still cry from missing the everydayness of us and the brutal truth of his death's finality. But, in the end, Peter did die, and he will never come back. How he died is no longer important. Wishing him back won't make it so. Peter is gone and will remain gone. As painful as that admission is, nothing will change any of that. Nothing. I am still here. My sadness can come any time it wants, but it can't stay, not while I keep living.

What Else Am I Supposed to Do?

My mother didn't have an easy life. She had seven children in eleven years with three miscarriages, took care of my father riddled with heart disease all of my life, and worked full-time during a period in our history when not many mothers were in the job force. She was an amazing woman who juggled so much in her life and did so without complaint. When I complimented more than a few times about her strength and grace in handling it all, she would pass it off with a shrug and a question of, "What else was I supposed to do?" She wasn't wrong. What else was she supposed to do? Giving up was not an option.

I have been thinking about my mother lately. Like many daughters, there are jarring moments of I-am-my-mother that hit me like a wrecking ball, knocking me on my ass. It's not because it's something to be shameful of or even angry about, but sometimes, it just shocks me. I consider my mother one of the strongest people I have ever known. When I get glimpses of her in me, especially now in widowhood, I can't believe I have it. I wonder if there was a gene she handed down to me, a tough, resilient one she had in her from our ancestors. I suppose it doesn't matter. All that does is that she lives in me, and the other night, I recognized her spirit in me.

It came after a night of trying out a new grief group. After an hour and a half of meditating—okay, me *trying* to meditate—and thinking about my life now, I realized the number of emotions I have gone through before, during, and after Peter's death. It was a shocking revelation that had me reeling well into the night. To say the past year and a half has been a rough one would be stating the obvious. While I should still be on the ground for all the events that pulled the rug out from underneath me, I am still standing. Not only standing, but moving—slowly, painfully, insecurely, sure, but moving, in part because of my mother.

It started when my daughter, the person who once gave me a magnet with a quote from the TV show *Gilmore Girls* about a mom being a best friend, moved five hours away to pursue her dreams. Three months later, my son moved out, as it was his time leaving me with a fully emptied out nest. A few weeks after my son's flight from the nest, I had a thyroidectomy due to a cancer scare. Two months later, as I finally settled into my idea of growing old together with my best friend, my lover, my companion, my growing older partner, and my co-parent, Peter died. Half of me died with him. Nine months later, still trying to recover from all the blows in the previous months, another punch opened up a still-healing life when my mother died. It seemed like just as I caught my breath, another blow was delivered to have me curled up again.

At almost ninety-two, my mother's death was not unexpected. It was, in fact, welcomed and wanted by her.

As much as I knew it was her time, the thought of never seeing her again, like Peter's death, tore open another part of my heart. Then, a week later, Life shot up its middle finger at me and brought on COVID, an entirely different type of loss altogether.

I reflected on all the bitch slaps life gave to me the other night during my attempt at meditation. I thought about my mother's shrug and the question of, "What else was I supposed to do?" She was right then and right now as it applies to me. What else *am* I supposed to do?

From the beginning of this nightmare, I have said there is no option B. There never will be one. I have to, want to, need to, forge ahead in life, figuring out how to navigate on this reluctant journey I'm on. The pain may slow me down, but I won't let it stop me.

Through my mother's example, I learned when life hands me struggles, permanent losses, and a crap-load of pain, I have to keep on keeping on in hopes it does get better. I have to lift my head and look to the horizon beyond all of the pain. I have to raise my eyesight to the light above the hell I slipped into and keep on moving forward.

My mother had a difficult life. In many ways, my life has started to resemble hers. I have her stubbornness to carry on. I can't, and she couldn't, succumb to life's shit. Like my hero, my mother, I will face it head-on. I will be the warrior she showed me to become, the warrior women of my ancestors. My mother's resilience, strength, and determination stream in my veins, live in my head, and stay in my heart.

I will have more *I-am-my-mother* moments. They are a great source of pride to me and education for me. When I can't stand or figure out where to step next, when all I want to do is climb in my bed and let the world pass, I will lift myself up in hope and move in the direction of living. With my mother's shrug and question, "What else am I supposed to do?" I will know there is no option B. And, like my mother, I will keep on.

Visions on a Board

I finally got around to my vision board. With my grief becoming more manageable, I want to create one. I have done vision boards in the past, and I don't see them as magical. I see them as acknowledgments to the Universe about my focus in life, what I would like and need to accomplish. Like my vision board from last year, this one is not fancy. It's pretty vanilla, made up of a few pictures and words with basic themes of writing, my future, and health. However, four images on my board are very personal to me, reminding me how to keep on and succeed on this reluctant journey.

The first are words to remind myself that doubt and fear are okay in grief and each passing stage of grief. With my mother's death, COVID, and the ever-present grief of Peter's death, I have started to look deeper into relationships, decisions, my purpose, losing one half of myself while another takes its place, and being true to who I am now. I am reminded I am now a seeker of who I am, who I am to become, even while the reasons of Peter's death remain unanswered. As I regain more of my faith in God, I still hold doubts. As I grow more accepting of my life as it is now, I still question everything that has happened. Despite my doubts and questions, my active brain has kept me afloat and not let me drown in the sorrows of my soul.

The second image on my board that holds much meaning to me is a simple statement, "I am a writer." Too often, I have shied away from saying this about myself. My insecurity whispers to me that I am not good enough to admit this. It shouts that I am an imposter because I make little money off this. I grew uncomfortable labeling myself as a writer, almost feeling pompous to say this aloud. I feared the negative responses from others. It never felt comfortable to admit my profession. Now, I know, to the core of me, it is who I am. I am continually pushing myself to embrace this writer in me, attempting to ignore anyone else, the reviewers, what people may think.

I know now I cannot hold anyone's approval or recognition above my definition. I cannot live in fear of not receiving either. I know it has to come from within me to grow the writer planted inside of me. The knowing is easy. The practice is hard. See, I am not the best gardener of my own being. I am trying to learn, though, and understand I have ways to go. Part of my education is to see this reminder continually—I am a writer—when I flip open my laptop to write, and believe it. I want to embrace my authentic self without comparison or waiting for affirmation from others. To the soul of me, I am a writer. I need to tend to this to bloom as one.

The third grabber in my vision board is the words "I can't" with a pair of scissors cutting through the 't' to read "I can." When Peter died, the first thing I asked was, "How am I going to live without him?" It was a rhetorical question, one which held no real answers for me. If it did, I didn't want to hear them. I wasn't ready.

It was too big for me to grasp how I would live in a world without the person who navigated it for me, who I allowed to navigate it for me. I let go of Life's wheel long ago and allowed Peter to take it over. Now, I have to steer Life myself, with shaky hands of diminishing faith and unknown skills. I have my insecurities and the fear of losing some people along the way. People sometimes put you in a box, and when you burst out, they don't necessarily know how to react, especially if you blast out by one of Life's sudden surprises.

I have been uncomfortable in a box for some time, and I don't feel comfortable staying in it anymore. I need to find comfort in my exit, to know I can live outside of it. And so, this image of cutting out the 't' in the word "can't" reminds me every day, I am no longer the person I once was, and I can slay whatever is in front of me, become who I imagined, rely only on myself.

Finally, the fourth placement on my vision board is the words "Widow Strong." That's what I want to be— Widow Strong—which means the acceptance of my status in life. It's been a struggle to see myself as a widow because it means having to admit the finality of Peter's death, something my shock won't let me do. For a long time, part of me, the deceivingly protecting part, thought he would walk in the door after five o'clock, or I would see him gardening in the backyard. When I see pictures of him, my heart drops out of my being with the realization that's where his image will remain—in photographs. I am a widow now. I am not part of a couple. I am no longer a wife. I am a singular person with only my name on credit cards, bills, and wedding invitations. I am a widow now, and that's not going to change any time soon, if ever.

I want to embrace that part of me, like my brown eyes and dark hair. Embrace and exercise it, strengthen it. I want to carry pride with me to have loved and been loved by an incredible man. I want to allow my peacock feathers to show when I talk about being his wife until death departed us. I want to get to know my widow identity, and all that means, so I can be strong, Widow Strong. It's a powerful statement and one I need to see every day.

I finally completed my vision board yesterday. It's nothing fancy. There are no bells and whistles, no ribbons, no meticulously placed lettering. It just lies on my computer screen with reminders of who I want to become, what I need to embrace, and what I have to let go of to live my authentic life, new life, and emerged life. And I see these reminders on my vision board every time I flip open my laptop. They serve as my strength to continue living as a seeker, a writer, a confident woman, and a widow.

Letting Go of Old Me

A widow's social media group posed this question: *Do you miss the person you were when your spouse was alive?* Serious question, and one I often contemplate since Peter died. The easy and quick answer seems to be hell, yeah, I miss her. If I were still that person, it would mean Peter was still alive, and I want him alive again, more than anything. Beyond that obvious fact, I also knew who I was with Peter. After thirty-two years together, I knew our rhythm, my rhythm with him. I knew how to counter his every move and dance through life on both the smooth and rough patches. I knew the joy of making him laugh or even smile his crooked smile. I knew the uplifting tummy bubbles I felt when I was around him, still after all our years together. I knew how much one person does not necessarily complete you but adds to your being. I knew the security of him, of a couple. And so I knew and loved who I was with him. I miss the knowledge of me with him.

There are other things I would miss. I miss the laughter that came so quickly to her because her pain came and went, never stayed. I miss the person who had the simple joy of being in the presence of a best friend. I miss the person who relished in intimacy and the touch once so prevalent in her life. I miss the security I felt with Peter and knowing the future would be less scary with him in it. I miss the person who felt loved without condition, respected without thought, and understood without explanation. I miss the person who relied on the comfort and assurance of her husband, especially during these dark times when both are so needed. I miss the person who had companionship and a constant. And mostly, I miss the person who was married, and all that meant, including the growing old together. My quick, reflexive answer is yes. I miss the person who no longer has any of these things that made her who she was, how she loved, and what she accomplished.

Yet, I also have begun to learn more about the woman emerging without Peter. Sometimes, I think I am a fraud, choosing something contrary to who I once was, and it doesn't always feel comfortable or authentic. I am still in the process of trying on the different skins life offered me since Peter died, and some are more pleasant than others. The uncomfortable ones are steps outside the box I lived in for so long and feel uneasy about because of the mere newness. More and more, I surprise myself, pleasantly, by how easy decisions, actions, and slow emergence can be, and those are the times I try to remember the most. They are the times that allow me to shake off the insecurities and the agony of doing this all on my own.

The reality is my spouse is dead. Because of his death, I had to develop and allow the surfacing of a person coping without him. In the process, I have grown other parts of this emerging person that I would miss. I would miss the self-reliant person, the person who has learned to make decisions without feedback or compromise. I would miss the new, unique confidence this person has developed, separate from others' opinions and boosts. I would miss the person who has become proficient in rising after each fall and has become competent in catching herself with each stumble. I would miss the talks of *you got this* with herself and the strains on the shoulders with each needed pat on the back she gave herself. I would miss the way her mind works as she navigates, alone, through murky and dark roads. I would miss a growth different from what she ever experienced, ever knew possible. I would miss the opportunities and the examples of strength and perseverance she hopes she is giving her children. And I would miss this person's dawn in the absence of her husband.

Peter was a great guy. I don't know anybody who had a beef with him, disliked him, or spoke ill of him. He was a great husband, friend, lover, and father. There is so much to miss about him and who I was with him. Yet, I know he would be proud of the person I am becoming, the person he may have known I always had in me. Or perhaps the person he never saw coming yet would enjoy.

Here's the thing. With or without Peter, the core of me has not changed. Peter was part of my life's branches, but he was never my roots. I am still me, the gal with a million opinions, wacky sense of humor, ricocheting brain, and forever love for Peter. With or without Peter, that core of me remains. Aspects of me are not the same as the old me, and that's okay. I can miss the old me, but I can't let my longing for her impede the progress of the person I have become as I live on without Peter. I have to let go of who I was with him in order to grow and become who I am without him, because I will be without him for the rest of my life. I can't hold onto the dead parts of me and still expect to grow.

And so, I guess my final response to the question *do I miss the person I was when Peter was alive* is not a simple one, or a quick one, but an honest one. Sometimes, yes, but most times, I am too busy figuring out who I will become now that he›s dead.

I will never *get over* Peter's death. How can I? His death emptied a part of my soul that will never be filled up by anyone or anything. I will *move on,* though, with the unoccupied space his death left inside of me. I will allow myself to grieve and allow his memories, our memories, to be a part of who I am now. I will *not* allow myself to stand still, let the past permeate my future, ask for permission to move on, or always glance back while I move forward. I will continue to respect, love, honor, and miss what I was and what I had with Peter. I will do all of this while I become who I am meant to be now. I have to. I owe this to my kids, to Peter's memory, and most importantly, to myself.

Life is ever evolving. Sometimes it is not how we pictured it or what we asked for, and that seems so unfair. I was handed a horrible situation, one of the worse life can give anyone. I didn't know how I would continue living. Yet I did. I feel an excitement in my evolution because I have a story that needs to be told. My ending is not over.

The Eulogy

Getting through this time in widowhood taught me a lot about myself, my capacity to love, my ability to receive love, and the dormant strength in me. There were times I didn't think I would make it, and other times, I knew I would. All the time, I understood I had no choice but to keep moving. Another option did not exist for me. The longing for him, the living life without him, the inability to explain it all to people who have not walked on this path, the gratitude for friends and family, the anger held for too many reasons, the insecurity of being on my own, the aloneness, and the mirage of emotions I'm still unable to express, have been the most difficult part of life I ever lived. As I continue to move through the rest of my life without him, I am sharing Peter's eulogy from his memorial service. As you can imagine, it was a difficult eulogy to write and to give, and yet, like everything else I've accomplished since his death, I did it. I did the best I could to summarize Peter and his life, a life he spent the majority of with me, a union only broken when death did part us. Here it goes . . .

Thank you all for being here to celebrate Peter. All the outpour of phone calls, visits, texts, food—oh my word, the food—and posts on social media, reinforced what I already knew. my mister was a light in this world, a light suddenly blown out too soon and darkened our world.

This past week, there were so many words used repeatedly to define Peter—gentle, kind, humble, funny, dedicated, patient, loving, and of course, intelligent. He has been described as a man his nephews aspired to be, a man who stood out among the greatest, a man who could talk equally about electromagnetism and the Ramones. He was to many the best of friends, the finest of neighbors, and the most charitable of persons. I was told Peter was unassuming, likable, lovable, and a quiet man with warm smiles that reached his eyes.

Peter loved his five siblings, his many nieces and nephews, and the abundance of great nieces and nephews. He spoke often of his sister Bonnie taking care of him while his parents worked, and the trip to Colorado with his sister Sally and brother-in-law Bill. He spoke with pride about all the knowledge his brother Dan handed down to him about cars. He worried about his brother Tom's recent health battle. And of course, there was Peter's never-wavering adoration of, and commitment to his twin sister, Trisha.

It says a lot about a person when he holds onto his lifetime friends, and Peter's tight grip on his best ones, Larry, Leo, and Troy, spoke volumes. They were his constants for the past thirty-five to forty-five years. They loved him and he loved them like brothers.

Peter made his mark on the community and this world. He was an active and dedicated member of the Kiwanis Club, served on the local education district's Citizen

Advisory Committee and the local Arts Council board.
He helped cleaned up parks, assisted in prairie burns, and
volunteered at events for the Park District. He supported
the local high school's marching band in numerous ways,
even years after our daughter graduated. He was a teacher
and active promoter for Sail Chicago. He volunteered to
record data for the Forest Preserve's bluebird population,
even making bluebird boxes when some were destroyed
by storms. And, because he was Peter, he placed dollar
bills on his car's visor to hand out to the distraught he
saw on the street, something I didn't know about for years
because of Peter's humility. Peter's list of selfless acts could
go on and on, but these are just some snapshots of a man
with an impressive highlight reel.

My son has already given a beautiful testimony to
Peter's strength as a father. Not more I can add, except
to say without Peter as my co-parent, our children would
not be the gold that shines so strong today. As far as my
own thoughts of Peter, the best way I can describe our
twenty-eight-year marriage and thirty-two-year relation is
he was the yin to my yang.

A few days before he died, Peter and I had one of
those stupid fights husbands and wives often have, one of
those you-didn't-tell-me-you-didn't-listen fights. We held
our ground for about a day, rehashing our own insistence
again and again. We finally sat down to make peace,
with both of us still hanging on to our stances. Finally,
Peter said to me, "You know, Betsy, I am precise, and
my livelihood is based on accuracy. You are this creative
person who writes stories with characters, so you have

all these voices in your head. Sometimes, you think you say things, but really, you're saying it in your head, not aloud."

I don't know if anything was really resolved, but I do know I was over the moon happy he thought I was creative . . . ignoring the fact he also thought I heard voices in my head.

This argument was a perfect example of us and of the yin and yang in our twenty-eight-year marriage, our thirty-two-year relationship. Peter kept me grounded when I needed it, while I brought him into the clouds when he deserved it. My anxiety-ridden-self ruminated on the "what-ifs," and Peter's calm demeanor countered with "what-if-nots."

Peter was my organized, precise, holding-close-his-emotions husband. I was his where-did-I-put it, scattered, heart-on-my-sleeve wife. He put things in files, I stuffed things in drawers. His conversations stayed on track, mine jumped the rails. He was the tranquility in my life, and I was the frenzy that made him laugh. It worked for us. It worked well for us. We gave to each other what was missing in ourselves, and that's how we became whole.

Peter lived his first eighteen years in a small town surrounded by cornfields, with a then population of 18,000. For his last twenty-four, he lived in a small town, surrounded by suburbs with a population of 14,000. He began and ended his life in small towns where his heart was planted. It seems only fitting, his life went full circle. A circle he lived in without fear, without regrets, without hesitation, and with so much greatness.

I will miss the man who I chose and who chose me to live the rest of our lives together while creating two beautiful children. Goodbye Peter, my very best friend, my yin, my lover, and my mister.

Sometimes, we can't choose the paths life and death pave for us. We *can* choose how we move along them.

Peace in your nows.

Photo © Lisa Howard

Acknowledgement

During the anger stage of my grief, I concentrated heavily on those who let me down when Peter first died. Now, I replace my resentment with overwhelming gratitude for the many who came running through the explosion of despair and remained through the fallout. Besides the fabulous women I mentioned in my dedication, and of course Peter—who loved me, and I loved until death departed us—there are others I need to acknowledge and thank. Without them, *See Me Grieve* would not be written.

First and foremost, my deepest gratitude goes to my children, Leah and Matthew. You have been my voices of reason during the chaos, my steps when I could not move, my shelters through the storm, and my forever heartbeats. Thank you seems so weak, yet I offer it to you both, along with everything I am. You gave me purpose to live through the unlivable and showed me the joys to continue living.

Without my late mother, Gloria Tobolski, I may not have made it through this journey. She was my example of fortitude and strength. Her life showed me how to keep on through the hard times with whatever I have in me. Thank you, Mumzy, for your uncanny wisdom and being the model of perseverance. I love you and miss you.

You would not be holding this book in your hands without the help of a gifted young editor, Nic Rueth. Your brilliance helped me grow as a writer, and your insight challenged me to become a better one. Thank you for understanding my story, questioning me when it was unclear, and at times, straightening out the words of a scattered mind.

See Me Grieve was able to get out into the world because of the talent at Ten16 Press. To my publisher and friend, Shannon Ishizaki; editor, Jenna Zerbel; interior layout, Lauren Blue; and cover designer, Kaeley Dunteman, thank you for your creativity, patience, kindness, seeing my vision, and incredible abilities to create specialness. It was a pleasure working with strong and capable women.

Thank you to my grief counselor, Laura. When stuck in the darkest of tunnels, you brought me to the light and showed me the hope. Thank you for helping me put my feelings into words and reminding me to celebrate all my small victories.

To Lisa and Monica, thank you for having big shoulders for me to cry on, laughter when I needed it, comfort during the difficulties, and understanding the impact from the loss of Peter. To all my Barkley Avenue neighbors, thank you for running when it all came down, doing without asking, and sharing your memories of Peter with me. You have all added to the fodder in this book.

Thank you to my Warrenville ladies, Brenda, Jill, and Tina. Our backyard get-togethers gave me the freedom to talk about my emptiness and helped my grief to move along. Thank you for always being interested in my stories, sharing laughs, and lending encouragement. Let's keep those group texts flying, gals.

In widowhood, the people who understand best are those in the same, reluctant club. Thank you to my special friend, Laura, for coming back into my life because of our common, widowed bond and never leaving. Thank you for your absolute grasp on all that is widowhood and your boundless compassion. Thank you to Sheila and Emily for reaching out with much of the same empathy.

For their unbelievable support while writing this book, I thank my writer friends, Alison, Cindy, Lynn A, Lynn W, and Norah. By always pointing out my strength, even when I didn't feel strong, expressing your interest in my writing, extending friendship, and recognizing the obstacles only fellow wordsmiths could know, you gave me the validation to write every day.

Thanks to family members who showed up for me. My gratitude goes out to Fran and Glor for being the big sisters I needed you both to be, and to Cheri, who has always been a friend first, a sister-in-law second, for spending some of my earliest, darkest times with me. Thank you to my Dudak family—Bonnie, Dan, Sally, and Trish—for the times you put your grief for your beautiful brother aside to focus on me. Your selflessness will forever touch me. Thanks to my nephews and nieces, the ones who reached out with kind words and offers of help for my kids and me. I thank all of you.

Thanks to Tina, Ted, and Geoff for helping me comprehend the financial language I never spoke or understood, and to doing so with stamina, compassion, and humor. Thank you for getting me from the moment we met, and for our developing friendships.

Thank you to Diane, who was on this journey from the beginning, understanding my reluctance to let go and being patient with me until I could. I appreciate your talent and our deepening connection because of it. You were part of the making of my new life, which includes writing this book.

Thank you to Patt and Judi for all the greeting cards you sent me in the months after Peter died. There were so many times where I needed your words to carry on. Your kindness will never be forgotten. Thank you to Patti, who seemed to know just the right time to send an encouraging text.

Thank you to the town I live in and all the people in it for being the comforting arms I needed around me. After Peter died, I couldn't live anywhere else except in the place that held my heart, my beloved Warrenville. It is here where I wrote this book.

Thank you to all my social media friends, too many to mention, who supported me and my writing through this entire journey. Thank you especially to the ladies of the Academy—you know who you are—and all my past and present friends for your consistent words of support. Every word of inspiration, powerful comments of optimism, social media hugs, and private messages of reassurance were the catalysts in starting and completing this book.

And finally, to my dog, Barkley, and my grand-pup, Lily. You two fur buddies give me so much joy and purpose. Thank you for the chuckles I needed when this book became too much for me.

CPSIA information can be obtained
at www.ICGtesting.com
Printed in the USA
LVHW081441210621
690308LV00004B/6